Henry Arthur Bright

**A Year in a Lancashire Garden**

Henry Arthur Bright

**A Year in a Lancashire Garden**

ISBN/EAN: 9783337068875

Printed in Europe, USA, Canada, Australia, Japan

Cover: Foto ©Andreas Hilbeck / pixelio.de

More available books at **www.hansebooks.com**

# A YEAR IN A LANCASHIRE GARDEN.

# A YEAR

IN A

# LANCASHIRE GARDEN

BY

HENRY A. BRIGHT

London
MACMILLAN AND CO.
AND NEW YORK
1891

*The Right of Translation is Reserved*

RICHARD CLAY AND SONS, LIMITED,
LONDON AND BUNGAY.

*First Edition*, May, 1879.   *Reprinted*, August, 1879; 1891.

# PREFACE.

THIS volume is but a collection of Notes, which, at the request of the editor, I wrote, month by month, in 1874, for the columns of the *Gardeners' Chronicle.*

They pretend to little technical knowledge, and are, I fear, of but little horticultural value. They contain only some slight record of a year's work in a garden, and of those associations which a garden is so certain to call up.

As, however, I found that this monthly record gave pleasure to readers, to whom both the garden and its owner were quite unknown, I printed off some fifty copies to give to those, whom I have the happiness to number among my friends, and for whom a garden has the same interest that it has for me.

Four years have passed since then, and I am still asked for copies which I cannot give.

I have at last, rather reluctantly, for there seems to me something private and personal about the whole affair, resolved to reprint these notes, and see if this little book can win for itself new friends on its own account.

One difficulty, I feel, is that I am describing what happened five years ago. But this I cannot help. To touch or alter would be to spoil the truthfulness of all. The notes must stand absolutely as they were written. But after all, I believe, the difficulty is only an apparent one. The seasons, indeed, may vary—a spring may be later, a summer may be warmer, an autumn may be more fruitful,—but the seasons themselves remain. The same flowers come up each year, the same associations link themselves on to the returning flowers, and the verses of the great poets are unchanged. The details of a garden will alter, but its general effect and aspect are the same.

Nevertheless, something has been learnt, and something remembered, since these notes were written, and this, also communicated from time to time to the *Gardeners' Chronicle*, I have condensed into a supplementary chapter.

If, as I have heard from a friendly critic, there is too much *couleur de rose* in my descriptions, I am tempted to retort that this is a colour not perhaps altogether inappropriate to my subject; but, be this as it may, I have described nothing but as it really appeared to me, and I have only wished that others should receive the same impressions as myself.

For my very open egotism I make no apology; it was a necessity of the plan on which I wrote.

I have added notes on the Roman Viola, and on the Sunflower of the Classics, and have given some extracts respecting the Solanum and the fly-catching Azalea. I have also reprinted, by the editor's kind permission, part of an article of mine that appeared in the *Athenæum* on "Flowers and the Poets."

# CONTENTS.

## I.

|  | PAGE |
|---|---|
| Introductory—The House—The Latest Flowers—The Arbutus—Chrysanthemums—Fallen Leaves — Planting — The Apple-room—The Log-house—Christmas ... ... | 1 |

## II.

Gardening Blunders—The Walled Garden and the Fruit Walls—Spring Gardening—Christmas Roses—Snowdrops—Pot Plants ... ... ... ... ... 10

## III.

Frost—The Vineries and Vines—Early Forcing—Orange Trees—Spring Work—Aconites—The Crocus ... ... 18

## IV.

The Rookery—Daffodils—Peach Blossoms—Spring Flowers—Primroses—Violets—The Shrubs of Spring ... ... 26

## V.

The Herbaceous Beds—Pulmonaria—Wallflowers—Polyanthus—Starch Hyacinths—Sweet Brier—Primula Japonica—Early Annuals and Bulbs—The Old Yellow China Rose ... ... ... ... ... ... ... 34

## VI.

Ants and Aphis—Fruit Trees—The Grass Walk—"Lilactide"—Narcissus—Snowflakes—Columbines—Kalmias—Hawthorn Bushes ... ... ... ... ... 42

## VII.

The Summer Garden—The Buddleia—Ghent Azaleas—The Mixed Borders—Roses—The Green Rose ... ... ... 51

## VIII.

The Fruit Crop—Hautbois Strawberries—Lilium Auratum—Sweet Williams—Carnations—The Bedding-out ... ... 59

## IX.

Weeds—Tomatos—Tritomas—Night-scented Flowers—Tuberoses—Magnolia—Asters—Indian Corn ... ... ... 67

## X.

St. Luke's Summer—The Orchard—The Barberry—White Haricot Beans—Transplanting—The Rockery ... ... 75

## XI.

The Wood and the Withered Leaves—Statues—Sun-dials—The Snow—Plans for the Spring—Conclusion ... ... 82

## SUPPLEMENTARY CHAPTER.

Flowering Shrubs—Yuccas—Memorial Trees—Ranunculus—Pansies—Canna Indica—Summer Flowers—Bluets—Fruit blossoms and Bees—Strawberry Leaves—Garden Sounds—Mowing—Birds—The Swallow—Pleasures of a Garden   89

## NOTES.

I.—On the Viola of the Romans ... ... ... 107
II.—On the Azalea Viscosa ... ... ... 110
III.—On the Solanum Tribe ... ... ... 112
IV.—On the Sunflower of the Classics .. 115
V.—On Flowers and the Poets ... ... 118

# A YEAR IN A LANCASHIRE GARDEN.

# A YEAR IN A LANCASHIRE GARDEN.

## I.

Introductory—The House—The Latest Flowers—The Arbutus—Chrysanthemums—Fallen Leaves—Planting—The Apple-room—The Log-house—Christmas.

*December* 3.—These notes are written for those who love gardens as I do, but not for those who have a professional knowledge of the subject; and they are written in the hope that it may not be quite impossible to convey to others some little of the delight, which grows (more certainly than any bud or flower) from the possession and management of a garden. I cannot, of course, by any words of mine, give the hot glow of colour from a bed of scarlet Ranunculus with the sun full upon it, or bring out the delicious scent of those double Tuberoses, which did so well with me this autumn;

but I can at least speak of my plans and projects, tell what I am doing, and how each month I succeed or fail,—and thus share with others the uncertainty, the risks and chances, which are in reality the great charm of gardening. And then, again, gardening joins itself, in a thousand ways, with a thousand associations, to books and literature, and here, too, I shall have much to say.

Lancashire is not the best possible place for a garden, and to be within five miles of a large town is certainly no advantage. We get smoke on one side, and salt breezes on another, and, worst of all, there comes down upon us every now and then a blast, laden with heavy chemical odours, which is more deadly than either smoke or salt. Still we are tolerably open, and in the country. As I sit writing at my library window, I see, beyond the lawn, field after field, until at last the eye rests on the spire of a church three miles away.

A long red-gabled house, with stone facings, and various creepers trained round it,—a small wood (in which there is a rookery) screening us from a country road, and from the west,—lawns with some large trees and several groups of evergreens,—and the walled garden, the outer garden, and the orchard;—it is to these that I invite you. Exclusive of meadow-land there are only some four acres, but four acres are enough for many gardening purposes, and for very great enjoyment.

These are certainly what the American poet Bryant calls "the melancholy days, the saddest in the year." The late autumn flowers are over;—the early spring ones are still buried under the soil. I could only find this morning a single blighted monthly Rose, a Wallflower or two, an uneasy-looking Polyanthus, and some yellow Jasmine against the house—and that was all. Two days of early frost had killed the rest. Oddly enough, however, a small purple flower caught my eye on the mixed border; it was a Virginian Stock,—but what it was doing at this unwonted season who can say? Then, of course, the Arbutus is still in bloom, as it has been for the last two months, and very beautiful it is. There is a large bush of it just as you enter the walled garden, and, though the pink clusters of blossom are now past their best, they are more welcome than ever in the present dearth of flowers. Can any one tell me why my Arbutus does not fruit? It has only borne one single berry in the last four years; and yet the Arbutus fruits abundantly in other places in Lancashire, and at Lytham, close to the sea, I saw clusters of berries only the other day. Sometimes I fancy there is a better chance of the fruit setting if the pollen is from another tree, and I have lately planted a second Arbutus for the experiment. I am very fond of the Arbutus; it carries me back to the days of Horace, for we remember how his goats, wandering along the lower slopes of Lucretilis, would browse upon the thickets of Arbutus that fringed its side.

Lastly, the Chrysanthemums are in flower, though not in the inner garden. Some I have tended and trained, and they are now looking handsome enough in the porch and vestibule of the house. Some I have planted, and allowed to grow as they like, in front of the shrubbery borders; these have failed very generally with me this year—they look brown and withered, and the blooms are small, and the stems long and ragged, while many have entirely disappeared. The best of them all is Bob, with his bright, red, merry face, only surpassed by a trained Julia Lagravière in the porch. Another favourite Chrysanthemum of mine is the Fleur de Marie, with its large white discs, all quilled inside and feathered round the edge. Fastened up against a wall, I have seen it, year after year, a mass of splendid snowy blossom. The Chrysanthemum has three merits above almost every flower. It comes in the shortest and darkest days; it blooms abundantly in the smoke of the largest cities; it lasts longer than any flower when cut and put into water. If flowers have their virtues, the virtue of the Chrysanthemum is its unselfish kindliness.

In the outer garden, we have been busy with the fallen leaves, brushing them away from the walks and lawn, leaving them to rot in the wood, digging them into the shrubbery borders. This work is finished now, and we have swept up a great stack for future use at the end of two years. The Beech and the Oak leaves we (in opposition to some authorities) hold to be the most valuable, but of course we cannot keep them distinct from the rest. These fallen leaves—of which we make our loam for potting purposes—what endless moralities they have occasioned! The oldest and the youngest poets speak of them. It is Homer, who compares the generations of men to the generations of the leaves, as they come and go, flourish and decay, one succeeding the other, unresting and unceasingly. It is Swinburne, who says in his poems—

> "Let the wind take the green and the grey leaf,
>   Cast forth without fruit upon air;
> Take Rose-leaf, and Vine-leaf, and Bay-leaf
>   Blown loose from the hair."

During this open weather we have been getting on with our planting. Those beds of Rhododendrons just under the drawing-room windows have become too thick. They are all good sorts—John Waterer, Lady Emily Cathcart, and the rest—and must have sufficient room. We move a number of them to the other side of the house, opposite the front door, where till now there has been a bed of the common Rhododendrons, and this in turn we plant as a fresh bed elsewhere.

There will be now some space to spare in the hybrid beds, and I shall plant in them a number of roots of the Lilium candidum—the dear old white Lily of cottage gardens. They will come up each year from between the Rhododendrons, and will send their sweet subtle odour through the open windows into the house. And as I write I am told of a recipe showing how, in the Wort-lore of old, the firm white petals were esteemed of use. You must gather them while still fresh, place them unbroken in a wide-necked bottle, packed closely and firmly together, and then pour in what brandy there is room for. In case of cut or bruise no remedy, I am told, is more efficacious, and certainly none more simple.

*December* 23.—The weather is still mild and open. We have had three days' sharp frost, but it soon passed, and, while it lasted, it spared even the Chrysanthemums. "Bob" looks better than ever. During the frost was the time to look over the Apple-room, the Mushroom-bed, and the Log-house.

The Pears we are now using are the Winter Nelis, which I believe is known also as the Bonne de Malines. It is a capital Pear at this season of the year, and in these parts, and trained on my south-west walls, bears well, though the trees are young. I only planted them some four years ago, and, as all the world knows,—

"You plant Pears
For your heirs."

The Mushrooms are late this year; the spawn appeared less good than usual, and I expected a total failure, but, after all, there is promise of a dish for Christmas Day. I do not care to grow Mushrooms when the green vegetables are in full glory but now they are very welcome.

As for the Log-house, it is full. We have cut down several trees, and huge Yule logs lie in heaps, ready for the hall fire. We shall want them before the winter is over. If Horace had to say to Thaliarchus in Italy (this is Lord Denman's version)—

> "Dissolve the cold, while on the dogs
> With lavish hand you fling the logs,"—

surely in these northern latitudes, and in this dearth of coal, the advice is doubly seasonable. And then a log fire is so charming. It does more than warm and blaze—it glows and sparkles. But Mr. Warner, the American, has just given us in his *Backlog Studies* long pages about wood-fires, and I need only refer to that very pleasant little book. One quotation, however, I will give :—

> "We burn in it Hickory wood, cut long. We like the smell of this aromatic forest timber and its clear flame. The Birch is also a sweet wood for the hearth, with a sort of spiritual flame, and an even temper—no snappishness. Some prefer the Elm, which holds fire so well; and I have a neighbour who uses nothing but Apple-tree wood—a solid, family sort of wood, fragrant also, and full of delightful associations. But few people can afford to burn up their fruit-trees."

But besides the dead wood, we have just cut our fresh Christmas boughs. Up against an outhouse I have an immense Ivy, almost as large as one you see growing up some old castle: it spreads along the wall, covering it all over on both sides; then it climbs up a second wall at right angles to the first, and throws its trailing branches down to the very ground: and now they are one mass of blossom.

It is from this ivy that we gather our best Christmas greenery; but there are also cuttings from the Box, Yew, and Holly;—and one variegated Holly has been beautiful, for its mottled leaves have in some sprays become of a perfectly clear and creamy white—the colour of fine old ivory. Mistletoe does not grow with us, and we have to buy it in the market of our town. By the way, how strangely the idea of an English Mistletoe bough now associates itself with that very uncomfortable Italian story of the bride and the oaken chest. How curious, too, that, in this country at least, the memory of poor Ginevra is due not to Rogers's poem, but to Haynes Bayly's ballad.

To-morrow will be ·Christmas Eve, and to-morrow (so the legend says), in the vale of Avalon, —at the old abbey, where King Arthur was buried and St. Dunstan lived—"outbuds the Glastonbury Thorn"—the sacred Thorn, which sprang from the staff St. Joseph planted there. Unhappily no such Thorns grow in my Lancashire garden.

## II.

*Gardening Blunders—The Walled Garden and the Fruit Walls—Spring Gardening—Christmas Roses—Snowdrops—Pot Plants.*

*January* 5. — What wonderful notions some people have about gardens! In a clever novel I have just been reading, there occurs this description :—" The gardens at Wrexmore Hall were in a blaze of beauty, with Geraniums and Chrysanthemums of every hue." In the published letters of Mr. Dallas, who was formerly United States' Minister here, there is something still more marvellous. He had been staying with Lord Palmerston at Broadlands in the end of September, and he speaks of "the glowing beds of Roses, Geraniums, Rhododendrons, Heliotropes, Pinks, Chrysanthemums." I shall have to make a pilgrimage to Broadlands. Meanwhile, why should we not more often bed out Chrysanthemums in masses, as in the Temple Gardens? A "winter garden" is generally nothing more than a garden of small evergreens, which, of course, is an improvement on bare soil, but which is in itself not singularly interesting.

Since last I wrote, we have had storms of wind and rain, and some little snow and frost, but the weather has, on the whole, been very genial for the time of year. I have finished my planting, and am now busy re-sodding the grass terrace which runs along the south and east of the house; the grass had become full of weeds, and in places was bare and brown. But my most important work has been within the walled garden. This garden is entered by a door in the south-east wall, and two walls, facing south-west and north-east, run at right angles to it. A thick hedge, guarded by wire netting to keep out the rabbits, is at the further or north-west side, and divides us from the home-croft. Along the south-east wall we have two vineries, and between them a small range of frames and hotbeds. Against the sheltered wall between the vineries we have a Magnolia grandiflora, which flowered with me last year; a Banksian Rose, which has done no good as yet; and a Général Jacqueminot, which is always beautiful. A Camellia (Woodsii), which flowered abundantly last spring, I have moved elsewhere, and have planted a Maréchal Niel in its place. Beyond the vineries on both sides are my best Peaches and Nectarines. On the south-west wall are Peaches and Nectarines, Apricots, Plums and Pears, and on the north-east Cherries and Currants. In front of the Vine border is a broad gravel walk, which reaches along the whole breadth of the garden, and on the other side of it are the flower-beds. There are about forty of them in all, of different shapes and sizes, and divided from each other by little winding walks of red Jersey gravel. As you come upon them all at once, but cannot see the whole at a glance, I have no temptation to sacrifice everything to monotonous regularity and a mere effect of colour. I take bed by bed, and make each as beautiful as I can, so that I have a constant variety, and so that at no season of the year am I entirely bare of flowers. Box hedges three feet high and some two and a half feet thick, and a screen of Rhododendrons, separate the flower garden from the kitchen garden, which is beyond; and right through both flower garden and kitchen garden, from the front of the Vine border to the far hedge by the croft, we have just been extending a grass walk, and planting, along the part that skirts the kitchen garden, Pears, Plums, and (for sake of a very uncertain experiment) a Walnut and a Medlar.

My spring gardening is on no great scale. A bed of mixed Hyacinths, another of single Van Thol Tulips, and another of Golden Prince Tulips, two beds of Wallflowers, one of red Daisies edged with white, and one of Polyanthus, are all I have at present planted. There will be more by and by. Meanwhile the spring flowers I really care about are those that come up every year on the mixed borders,—the outside borders of the flower garden. They are old friends that never fail us; they ask only to be left alone, and are the most welcome "harbingers of spring," bringing with them the pleasant memories of former years, and the fresh promise of the year that is to come.

I never saw such Christmas Roses as I have just now. Clustering beneath their dark serrated leaves rise masses of bloom,—bud and blossom,—the bud often tinged with a faint pink colour, the blossom a snowy white guarding a centre of yellow stamens. I have counted from thirty to forty blooms upon a single root, and I sometimes think the Eucharis itself is not a finer flower. The Christmas Rose, the Helleborus niger, has been celebrated by Pliny, by Spenser, and by Cowley; but I confess my own favourite association with it is of a later date. I never see it without recalling the description poor Anne Brontë gives in her strange wild story of *The Tenant of Wildfell Hall.* Just at the end, when Helen, after her sad unhappy life, is free at last, and wishes to tell Gilbert that what remains of her life may now be his, she turns to "pluck that beautiful half-blown Christmas Rose that grew upon the little shrub without, just peeping from the snow that had hitherto, no doubt, defended it from the frost, and was now melting away in the sun." And then, "having gently dashed the glittering powder from its leaves," she says, "This Rose is not so fragrant as a summer flower, but it has stood through hardships none of them could bear: the cold rain of winter has sufficed to nourish it, and its faint sun to warm it; the bleak winds have not blanched it, or broken its stem, and the keen frost has not blighted it. Look, Gilbert, it is still fresh and blooming as a flower can be, with the cold snow even now on its petals. Will you have it?" Nowhere in the whole of the Brontë novels (so far as I remember) is a flower described as this one is.

It is suggestive enough of dark and drowsy winter, that the two flowers which most enliven it should bear the deadly names of black Hellebore and winter Aconite (though, indeed, the Eranthis is itself allied rather to the Hellebores than to the Aconites); as yet, however, my Aconites are still below the sod.

*January* 20.—It is St. Agnes's Eve, and never was there a St. Agnes's Eve so unlike that one which witnessed the happy adventure of young Porphyro. *Then*

> "St. Agnes' Eve; ah! bitter chill it was;
> The owl, for all his feathers, was a-cold;
> The hare limped trembling through the frozen grass,
> And silent was the flock in woolly fold."

*Now* the weather is soft, and almost warm.

I always seem to connect the idea of a Snowdrop with St. Agnes; and Tennyson speaks of "the first Snowdrop of the year" lying upon her bosom. This year our first Snowdrop appeared on the 18th, and now each day brings out fresh tufts on the herbaceous borders, where the sun strikes most warmly. Another week will pass, and, under the Lime trees which shade the orchard, I shall find other tufts of the double variety, planted in bygone years I know not by whom, and now springing up half wild and quite uncared for. And these Snowdrops gave me a hint a year or two ago. I found that my gardener was in the habit of throwing away his old bulbs—Hyacinths and Tulips—which had served their turn and lived their season. There was, of course, no good in keeping them for garden purposes; but this throwing them away seemed sadly wasteful. We now, therefore, plant them in the orchard grass, and each year they come up half wild like the Snowdrops, and each year they will be more numerous and more effective. But the best way of growing Snowdrops is, I believe, on a lawn itself. I have planted several hundreds of them in groups and patches, in a corner, where I can see them from the library window. The green spears are now piercing the grass, and in a few days there will be a broken sheet of snowy white, which will last for at least a fortnight, and which, from a distance, will seem like the lingering relic of some snowdrift still unmelted by the sun.[1] By the way, was it not Mrs. Barbauld who spoke of the Snowdrop as "an icicle changed into a flower?" The conceit is not a particularly happy one, for the soft white petals have nothing in common with the hard sparkle of the icicle.

[1] As matter of fact, the Snowdrops were less abundant this year than they usually are.—Has it ever been noticed that the colour of the winter flowers, as that of the Arctic animals, is almost always white?

We have not been fortunate this winter with the pot-plants which we require for the house. The Primulas have been singularly shabby. We had got some white sand from an excavation in the road near us, and it seems to have checked the growth of several of our plants. The Roman Hyacinths, too, have done less well than usual with us. There was a gummy look about many of the bulbs, which made us fear at the time that they were not properly ripened, and the result has proved that we were right. For dinner-table decoration can anything be prettier at this season than small Orange-trees—Japanese Oranges, I think they are—laden with their wealth of green and golden fruit? I have only just taken to them, and certainly I have seen nothing of the kind I like so well.

## III.

*Frost—The Vineries and Vines—Early Forcing—Orange-trees—Spring Work—Aconites—The Crocus.*

*February* 6.—We have had no morning so beautiful this winter. A clear, bright frost is in the air, and on the grass, and among the trees. Not a spray but is coated with crystals, white as snow and thick as moss; not a leaf of Holly or of Ivy but is fringed with frosted fretwork. There is not a breath of wind, and the birds, that were singing yesterday, have all vanished out of sight. It is wonderfully beautiful while it lasts, but it will be over before night.

Meanwhile, I am thankful for any touch of frost, if it will only come now instead of later. It will help to kill some few of the eggs and larvæ, which, in the different form of noxious insects, will plague us through the summer. It will keep back the fruit-tree buds, which are sadly too forward, and which will run a poor chance unless they are checked betimes. The Apricots especially look almost ready to open, and I can see colour even on the Nectarines.

We are beginning to force our first vinery. The year before last we had renewed the Vine border, and last year we did not venture any forcing; this year I hope we may be repaid. Our Black Hamburghs are old Vines of rather a good sort, with fine large berries and very few stones. The Muscats—Canon Hall, Alexandria, and Troveren—are Vines which I planted some three years ago. In the same house there is also an old Syrian Vine, bearing big bunches, but otherwise worth but little.

In the second vinery are Black Hamburghs again, Black Princes, Grizzly Frontignan, and a Sweetwater,—all old Vines; and to these I have added a Mrs. Pince's Muscat, a Foster's Seedling, and a Madresfield Court. Both vineries are of old construction, with clumsy flues, and require a thorough re-arranging, which I must give them some day. Quite the best grape, so far as flavour goes, is, I contend, the Grizzly Frontignan, which has now comparatively gone out of fashion. The bunches, it is true, are not handsome, the berries are not large, and the colour is not good; but has any Muscat a finer or more aromatic flavour? It was Sir William Temple who first introduced it, and he speaks of it with pride as "the noblest of all Grapes I ever ate in England." The Sweetwater is of value in another way; it is of all Grapes the most grateful and refreshing to an invalid. Only the autumn before last I was asked by an old friend whether anywhere in our neighbourhood the Sweetwater was still grown. He had been very ill, and was longing for Grapes,—but the rich luscious Muscats, with their highly-flavoured and thickly-sugared juice, had been forbidden. He had searched in vain among the vineries of many great houses, where the Sweetwater has been long discarded, and it was a pleasant surprise to find that in my small vineries this once favourite old Grape could still be found.

We are now bringing on our Strawberries; the Duc de Malakoff and Sir Charles Napier are the two we are forcing this year. Last year we had Oscar as well, but we found it a bad hanger, the first fruit damping away if it were not at once gathered. We are forcing also French Beans, Fulmer's Forcing,—and Tomatos, the Orangefield Dwarf. The prettiest thing in our vinery is a large Orange-tree, laden with last year's fruit, and soon to be covered with this spring's flowers. The fruit itself is only good for preserving, but it is wonderfully handsome, and no Orange-tree could be more prolific. Surely the old plan of having a separate Orangery is dying out in England, except of course in the very stately places. Thirty or forty years ago I think these Orangeries were more common in gardens of less pretension. I recall one, half green-house, half summer-house, with its large sashed windows opening to a lawn—windows round which a dozen creepers twined and blossomed;—inside stood the great Orange-trees in their huge tubs, waiting till the full summer, when they would be arranged along the broad terrace walk—in themselves beautiful, and calling up a thousand fragrant memories of Southern France and Italy. Now, I generally see trimmed Bays or Laurels arranged in porcelain pots, looking at once shabby and artificial. Of course I do not suppose Oranges worth growing except (a rather large exception) for their beauty; with Lemons it is different —they are certainly worth growing,—but then they do best trained up against the back of a moderately heated house, and not moved out in summer.

*February* 22.—Since I wrote we have had the sharpest and keenest frost—sharper than we have had all the winter; and an east wind which at once dried and froze up everything. Now spring has come again, and (as Horace says) has "shivered" through the trees. The Elders are already unfolding their leaves, and a Lonicera is in freshest bud. I remember when, a few years ago, Mr. Longfellow, the American poet, was in England, he told me that he was often reminded by the tender foliage of an English spring of that well-known line of Watts, where the fields of Paradise

"Stand dressed in *living green*;"

and I thought of this to-day when I looked, as I remember he was looking, at the fresh verdure of this very Lonicera.

But all things are now telling of spring. We have finished our pruning of the wall-fruit; we have collected our pea-sticks, and sown our earliest Peas. We have planted our Ranunculus bed and gone through the herbaceous borders, dividing and clearing away where the growth was too thick, and sending off hamperfuls of Pæony, Iris, Œnothera, Snowflake, Japanese Anemone, Day Lily, and many others. On the other hand we have been looking over old volumes of Curtis's *Botanical Magazine*, and have been trying to get, not always successfully, a number of old forgotten plants of beauty, and now of rarity. We have found enough, however, to add a fresh charm to our borders for June, July, and August.

On the lawn we have some Aconites in flower. They are planted at the foot of two great Beech trees, and last year they lay there—a soft yellow light upon the grass. This year they are doing badly. I suspect they must have been mown away last spring before their tubers were thoroughly ripe, and they are punishing us now by flowering only here and there. I know no flower so quaint as this—the little yellow head emerging from its deeply-cut Elizabethan ruff of green. Then, too, the Crocuses are bursting up from the soil, like Byron's Assyrian cohorts, "all gleaming in purple and gold." Nothing is more stupid than the ordinary way of planting Crocuses—in a narrow line or border. Of course you get a line of colour, but that is all, and, for all the good it does, you might as well have a line of coloured pottery or variegated gravel. They should be grown in thick masses, and in a place where the sun can shine upon them, and then they open out into wonderful depths of beauty. I am afraid Dr. Forbes Watson's most charming book on *Flowers and Gardens* is too little known. No modern author, not even excepting Ruskin, has studied the form and the beauty of flowers so closely and lovingly as he has done, and he entirely bears out my view. He says—

> "This is one of the many plants which are spoilt by too much meddling. If the gardener too frequently separates the offsets the individual blooms may possibly be finer, but the lover of flowers will miss the most striking charms of the humbler and more neglected plant. The reason is this: the bloom, when first opening, is of a deeper orange than afterwards, and this depth of hue is seemingly increased where the blossoms are small from crowded growth. In these little clusters, therefore, where the flowers are of various sizes, the colour gains in varieties and depth, as well as in extent of surface, and vividness of colour is the most important point in the expression of the yellow Crocus."

Besides the clusters along the shrubberies and the mixed borders, I have a number on the lawn beneath a large weeping Ash; the grass was bare there, and, though this is hidden in summer by the heavy curtains of pendent boughs and crowding leaves, it was well to do something to veil its desolation in the spring. Nothing can be more successful than a mass of Crocus, yellow, white, and purple.

I sometimes think that the Crocus is less cared for than it deserves. Our modern poets rarely mention it; but in Homer, when he would make a carpet for the gods, it is of Lotus, Hyacinth, and Crocus; and Virgil's bees find their honey among Cassia and Lime blossoms, and "iron-grey Hyacinths and glowing Crocus." Virgil speaks, too, of the scent of the Crocus (whatever that may be), and all Latin authors, when they wish to express a bright deep orange colour, call it the colour of the Crocus.

Our cool vinery is now gay with stages of Narcissus, Tulips, and Hyacinths, which have been brought on in heat, and are well rewarding us for what care we have given to them.

## IV.

*The Rookery—Daffodils—Peach Blossoms—Spring Flowers—Primroses—Violets—The Shrubs of Spring.*

*March* 6.—We have a tradition, or, if you will, a superstition, in this part of the world, that rooks always begin to build on the first Sunday in March. Last year my rooks were punctual to a day. This year, although they began a day or two earlier, it was not till the morning of Sunday the 1st that they showed real activity. Then the belt of trees which they frequent, and which for want of any better name we call "our wood," was all alive and clamorous. These rooks are only with us from March to the end of May, and then they are off again for the rest of the year to the woods which cluster thickly round the stately hall of the great nobleman of our county. But they never quite forget their nests among our Elms; and it is pleasant to see them in summer, and oftener still in late autumn, winging their way across the fields, and then wheeling down upon the trees. Who was it, who so happily applied to rooks the lines from the sixth Æneid, where Virgil, speaking of the descent of Æneas and his guide upon the Elysian plains, says

> "Devenere locos lætos, et amœna vireta
> Fortunatorum nemorum, sedesque beatas"?

> "And down they came upon the happy haunts,
> The pleasant greenery of the favoured groves—
> Their blissful resting-place."

There are many secrets about the rooks which I can never solve. Why do they build in the Elm rather than the Beech? My best trees are Beeches, but there are only two nests in them, whereas in a single Elm there are no less than ten. Why, again, do the old birds prevent the young ones from building in some particular tree? Sometimes, no doubt, there may be an unhappy association of the past, as in a case mentioned in Hawthorne's *English Note Book*, where in a garden, which I took him to see, not very far from this, some nests were once destroyed in a clump of trees, and never since has nest been built there. Sometimes, I think, because the rooks like to reserve certain trees as storehouses, from whence to gather their sticks. Again, how far is rook-shooting good for a rookery? It is commonly believed that, if a certain number are not shot, the rooks will desert. Is this so, and, if so, what should be the proportion? I have some sixty nests, and I wish to keep about this number.

I have planted many wild Daffodils in the wood; they are now coming into flower, but they do not seem to flourish as they should. I am told that Daffodils do not do well under a rookery, but I hardly think this likely.

If, as I said last month, the Crocus has been neglected by English poets, the Daffodil has no right to complain. Some of the most charming lyrics in the language are connected with this flower. Who does not remember Herrick's

> "Fair Daffodils, we weep to see
> You haste away so soon;"

or Wordsworth's

> "Host of golden Daffodils
> Beside the lake, beneath the trees,
> Fluttering and dancing in the breeze"?

Jean Ingelow, too, in her *Persephone*, makes the Daffodil the flower which tempts the unhappy maiden from her companions as they ramble along the fields of Enna—

> "The Daffodils were fair to see,
> They nodded lightly on the lea,
> Persephone, Persephone !
> Lo ! one she marked of rarer growth
> Than Orchis or Anemone ;
> For it the maiden left them both
> And parted from her company.
> Drawn nigh she deemed it fairer still,
> And stooped to gather by the rill
> The Daffodil, the Daffodil."

The end of the story we all know right well, for "Perdita" told us long ago how Persephone let her Daffodils all fall "from Dis's waggon."

*March* 25.—Again we have had frost and snow, and this time it has done us harm. The early bloom of the Apricot has turned black, and our chance of a crop rests with the later buds. However, there are plenty still; and now, in words familiar to half the children of England, "the crimson blossoms of the Peach and the Nectarine are seen, and the green leaves sprout." Here our promise is not so good, and we have nothing like the bloom of last year; in fact, a crop of Peaches and Nectarines in the open air is very uncertain in this Lancashire climate, and many of my neighbours have given in entirely, and have taken to glass-houses. I still go on; but certainly last year, in spite of the show of blossom, was not encouraging. Whether it is the increase of smoke or of chemical works I cannot say, but formerly wall fruit answered far better in these parts than it does at present. It is remarkable, however, that Sir William Temple, writing just 200 years ago, objects to growing Peaches farther north than Northampton, and praises a Staffordshire friend for not attempting them, and "pretending no higher, though his soil be good enough, than to the perfection of Plums."

We have been busy renewing the Box edgings to our flower-beds where it was required. Last year we had carelessly laid down salt on the narrow walks to destroy some weeds, and it has injured a good deal of the Box; some injury, too, has been caused by the growth of several strong plants, which got out of bounds and smothered it. Our garden is not a good spring garden. The soil is cold and heavy, and the delicate spring flowers do not thrive; but, on the other hand, no garden about is a better summer garden. It is a regular sun-trap, and yet even in the hottest weather the plants keep fresh and unburnt. Meanwhile the white Scilla, the double Daffodil, the Arabis, and some others, are doing well enough. A bed of Daisies and another of Polyanthus are far from satisfactory. Hepaticas I have tried over and over again, and they always fail.

In front of one of the beds of evergreens on the lawn I planted some double Primroses—yellow, white, red, and lilac; some of them are showing their blossoms, but they are not vigorous. By the way, I found it very difficult to get these Primroses, and had to pay what seemed an excessive price for them. They are, I fear, among the old neglected flowers, which we run a good chance of losing altogether, if gardeners will confine themselves entirely to bedding plants.

There is a charmingly fantastic conceit in one of Herrick's poems, "To Primroses filled with Morning Dew." He thinks they may be weeping, because

> "Ye have not seen as yet
> The Violet."

My Primroses at least have not this excuse, for we have Violets in abundance, and they scent all the air as we pass through the garden door. Even in winter a faint fragrance lingers among their leaves —a shadowy memory of a perfume, which haunts them even when no single flower can be found. Bacon says that "the flower which above all others yields the sweetest smell in the air is the Violet;

specially the double white Violet which comes twice a-year: about the middle of April and about Bartholomew-tide." Where is the double white Violet grown now?

One of the greatest floral heresies of modern days is as regards the Violet. Both Ruskin and Lord Stanhope have asserted that the Violet of the Greek and Latin poets was an Iris! If so, we are to believe that Athens was crowned with Iris; that the revellers at banquets decked themselves with wreaths of Iris; that wine was flavoured with Iris juice; and that a Violet is nowhere mentioned! Fortunately, however, Pliny makes it clear that there were Violets and Irises both, in old classic times; and the city of the Violet-crown is fragrant as of yore.[1]

Some of the flowering shrubs are now coming out and looking gay. There is the Mezereon with its upright shoots, all purpled over with their blossom; there is the Rhododendron dauricum with its beautiful lilac bloom; there, the oldest favourite of all, is the Pyrus japonica, with its bunches of cherry-coloured flowers, breaking out all along the hard-twisted branches. This Pyrus

---

[1] See note I. on the Viola of the Romans.

is no doubt most effective when trained up against a wall, and then, of course, it flowers earlier; but one bush of it is quite worth growing in any garden.

The last bit of planting we have done this year is an addition to our flowering-trees. We have got two of the best Robinias—the glutinosa and the hispida—and I shall be much disappointed if they do not prove a great success.

## V.

The Herbaceous Beds—Pulmonaria—Wallflowers—Polyanthus—Starch Hyacinths—Sweet Brier—Primula Japonica—Early Annuals and Bulbs—The Old Yellow China Rose.

*April* 4.—Is any moment of the year more delightful than the present? What there is wanting in glow of colour is more than made up for in fulness of interest. Each day some well-known, long-remembered plant bursts into blossom on the herbaceous borders, and brings with it pleasant associations of days that are no more, or of books that cannot die. It is, I think, Alphonse Karr who says we should watch closely and rejoice greatly over the slow procession of the flowers, as one by one they appear, bloom, and fade; if we are past middle life, it is a sight which, at best, we can only see some twenty or thirty times again.

The common double Daffodils are already past, but we have still the variety which, from its blended hues of dark orange and pale citron, the children call—as they call the wild Linaria—" the butter-

and-egg flower." Here is the Saxifraga crassifolia, with its huge broad leaves and its thick spikes of pink bell-blossom. It is almost too coarse growing, however, for the border, and does better on a rude rockery, or rather "loggery," which I have elsewhere.

Here is the Pulmonaria or Lungwort, with its varied bloom of red and blue, and with the white markings on its leaves, which were supposed to look like lungs, and from which it takes its name. This Pulmonaria is one of the large class of plants, which, it was believed, had a healing power, and indicated that healing power by the form of leaf, or root, or blossom. These herbs of grace—and it is doubtful whether any plant would be entirely excepted— bore about with them, plain for all to see, outward and visible signs of their secret and subtle virtue. Thus the Liverwort (Hepatica) had the shape of a liver in its leaves, the Eyebright (Euphrasia) looked up to you with an eye like your own—and each had potency of healing for that part of the human body, of which the image was expressed in its own frail form.

Farther on are close green tufts of the Corydalis, with its delicate lilac flowers. Then come bushes of Wallflower of the richest red-brown colour—a colour like nothing else, and indeed without a name, that would convey the depth and beauty of the dark tawny hue. What a contrast to the little wild yellow flower, which draws its scanty life from the wall of some grey old castle like that of Conway! Few scents are more delicious than that of Wallflowers. Bacon says of them that they "are very delightful, to be set under a parlour or lower chamber window." It is an old controversy whether the Wallflower and the Gillyflower are the same; but it seems tolerably clear that the latter name was rather loosely used, and meant sometimes the Wallflower, but sometimes also the Stock or the Clove Carnation. The Polyanthus on the borders has done better than those on the separate bed; the pretty *tortoise-shell* blossoms (to use a good expression of Forbes Watson) are just now in full perfection, and I have also a perfectly white Hose-in-hose Polyanthus, which is really charming. There is a droll passage in one of Sterne's love-letters to his future wife, in which he says—and he means to be sentimental and pathetic—

"The kindest affections will have room to shoot and expand in our retirement.—Let the human tempest and hurricane rage at a distance, the desolation is beyond the horizon of peace. My L. [the lady's name was Lydia] has seen a Polyanthus blow in December!

Some friendly wall has sheltered it from the biting wind.—No planetary influence shall reach us but that which presides over and cherishes the sweetest flowers."

There is still one other flower of which I must speak. It grows so abundantly, it flowers so luxuriantly with me;—it comes up like a weed on almost every border, and I have given it one entire bed to itself. It is the Starch or Grape Hyacinth, known also, I believe, as the Plum or Cluster Hyacinth. Its lower bells are of the darkest indigo, but towards the top it melts into the softest sky-blue tints, and when in masses it is beautiful. Ruskin says it is "as if a cluster of Grapes and a hive of honey had been distilled and compressed together into one small boss of celled and beaded blue."

Upon the wall by the vinery a Corchorus (Kerria) japonica is laden with wreaths of golden blossom. An Almond-tree near the front door is just shedding its pink petals. The double Gorse will be in flower in a week. But after all there is no flowering shrub, which we care for more just now than the still unflowering Sweet Brier. Towards the end of the walled garden I have laid out a miniature herb garden, with its separate little beds for Thyme and Marjoram, and Sage and Borage, and the rest, and inclosed it within a hedge of Sweet Brier. This Sweet Brier is now in leaf, and, after rain especially, it fills all that corner of the garden with whiffs and snatches of sweetest perfume. The Sweet Brier is the true Eglantine of the poets, for though Milton seems to confound "twisted Eglantine" with the Honeysuckle, Shakspeare has it right, and Titania's bower is, as we all know,

> " Quite over-canopied with luscious Woodbine,
> With sweet Musk Roses, and with Eglantine."

By the way, is the Musk Rose still found in English gardens, and what is it? Two years ago I got, with infinite trouble, a root or two, but they have died down again, and I begin to doubt whether I shall ever know its scent—a scent which Bacon says comes next to the Violet in perfuming the garden's air.

*April* 25.—The stages in the cool vinery are now gay with Spiræas and Cinerarias. The Lilies of the Valley are over, but they have done exceedingly well this year. I wonder whether the Trillium grandiflorum or Canadian Wood-Lily is generally known. I believe it to be hardy, but it was new to me, and I had grown it in a pot in the vinery, and a very pretty little flower it is, with its three green leaves, its three green sepals, and its three white petals. I have grown in the same way, for the first time, the Primula japonica, and surely nothing can be more beautiful than its five circles of crimson blossoms, one whorl above another. I have been so pleased with it, that I have just given orders for an entire bed of it to be made, which shall remain permanently, and between the plants I am dropping in Gladiolus bulbs, so that the bed will be in beauty for many weeks.

As I have before explained, you can hardly see the various beds of my flower-garden at a glance, so that I can go to work independently of the effects of the colour produced by elaborate bedding out. To tell the truth, too, I am heartily weary of the monotony of modern gardens, with their endless Pelargoniums, Calceolarias, and Verbenas. Some few such beds I cannot of course dispense with, but I am always glad when I can *reclaim* a bed for permanent herbaceous plants, as in this case of the Primula japonica.

Another bed, I trust, may be successful in another way—it is a bed of the blue Nemophila insignis. Two years ago I saw in the People's

Garden at Dublin, in the beginning of May, two beds, which struck me as being almost the most effective in their colouring of any I had ever seen. One was of Nemophila, the other of Virginian stock; one was a mass of the most brilliant blue, the other a blending of shades of tenderest lilac. The blooms were thick and close as possible, and the size of the flowers much finer than that of the ordinary spring-sown annuals. The manager of these gardens kindly explained to me his secret: the seeds were sown in autumn, pricked out in spring, protected during the early months, and then finally bedded out. Last year we tried with the Nemophila, but we were too soon, and the frost caught us and destroyed our plants. This year we are later, and, by giving some protection against cold and sun for a few days longer, I hope to reproduce what I saw in Dublin. Another year I may make trial of the Virginian Stock as well.

The Hyacinth bed has done fairly well, but there were too many pinks among the spikes for it to be quite successful. The Van Thol Tulips are a terrible failure. Some mice got to the bed, and, though we have killed thirteen of them, they had already eaten away so many of the crowns that some dozen Tulips, appearing here and there, are all I have. The bed of Golden Prince Tulips is, however, doing better; this always seems to me a very handsome Tulip, and I sometimes fancy has a sweetness of scent beyond all other kinds—a something, which at times half reminds one of the odour of some Tea Rose.

By the bye, I have had a Tea Rose in blossom in the vinery—of a sort I rarely see, and of which I really do not know the proper name. It used to grow over a cottage in Herefordshire, which I knew many years ago, and the Herefordshire nurseryman, from whom I got my standard, calls it "the old yellow China." Is this the right name, and is the Rose more common than I imagine? Its petals are loose and thin, and of a pale primrose colour, and before it is fully out it is at its best. Its leaves are large and handsome, and of glossy green. Its blossom has a certain half-bitter scent of Tea about it, to which the scent of no other Tea Rose can at all compare—it is so strong and aromatic.

We gathered our first forced Strawberries on the 16th; our first forced French Beans on the 17th, and our first Asparagus on April 18. This is early for us, but we are having the finest weather.

## VI.

Ants and Aphis—Fruit Trees—The Grass Walk—"Lilac-tide"—Narcissus — Snowflakes — Columbines — Kalmias — Hawthorn Bushes.

*May* 4.—May set in this year with (as Horace Walpole somewhere says) "its usual severity." We felt it all the more after the soft warm summer weather we had experienced in April. The Lilac, which is only due with us on the 1st of May, was this year in flower on the 28th of April. Green Gooseberry tarts, which farther south are considered a May-day dish, we hardly hope to see in this colder latitude for ten days later, and now these cold east winds will throw back everything.

I have been going over the fruit walls. The Apricots have, after all, done fairly well, and, if they do not fall off at the "stoning," we shall have nothing to complain of. Peaches and Nectarines are even worse than I had feared. There was not much bloom to begin with; then what bloom there was has set but badly; and now my most promising trees are overrun with aphis and with ants. We are doing everything that can be done to check the plague, but with only a partial success. I am told that ants do no harm, and, indeed, are useful as against the aphis. I do not know how this is. They seem to be most excellent friends, and the more ants there are the more the leaves curl up, and the more the aphis seems to thrive.[1] Last year one Peach-tree was completely killed, and this year two of them are looking very miserable. There has been no want of care or attention, but the enemy increases faster than we can destroy it. Is it a disease (so to speak) in a particular tree, which spreads to other trees? Or is it a blight in the air, against which we cannot guard? And what remedy is there when we have used tobacco-powder and Gishurst Compound, and all in vain?

Two Fig-trees against the wall, in the sunniest corners, are promising a full crop for this district; another Fig-tree of a smaller variety close by bears nothing. The old Arabic proverb, which

---

[1] I have since learned that the fact of the ant and the aphis being constantly together is well known; and further, that a sweet juice exudes from the aphis, on which the ant feeds. Pierre Huber declares that the aphis is the *milch-cow* of the ant; and adds, "Who would have supposed that the ants were a *pastoral people?*"

Emerson quotes, that "A Fig-tree looking upon a Fig-tree becometh fruitful," has not held good in this case. Lancashire, of course, is not the climate for Figs, but I should doubt whether Fig-trees are anywhere so common in England as they were 150 years ago, when Batty Langley of Twickenham wrote. He recommends them to be grown as dwarfs or standards as well as against a wall, and says they "are either white, black, yellow, grey, green, brown, purple, or violet-coloured, consisting of sixteen different kinds,"—but he adds that the white and the long purple do the best.

The Pears against the wall have but little fruit, but the standards are setting well, and the Apples will not, I hope, have suffered from this spell of cold. The new grass walk, of which I wrote on January 5 as passing right through the garden, is shaded by some Apple-trees, and it is pleasant to see their flakes of rosy snow falling softly on the fresh green beneath. Between these old Apple-trees and the young standards I have planted, there was room, which I am making ornamental with cones of Scarlet Runners. We have some five circles on each side of the walk, and shall train up the bean tendrils by strings fastened to a centre pole, so that in summer we shall have a succession of tents of scarlet and green. I tried this method of training Scarlet Runners on a smaller scale last year. The effect was excellent. Then, too, close along the grass on either side I am planting a broad belt of Violets, so that this new walk will one day be the sweetest part of the garden. Lastly, to give colour to the end of the walk, where it is bounded by the hedge of the croft, I am sowing the large Everlasting Pea, and the strongest growing Nasturtium, that they may climb and trail among the Hawthorn and the clipped Beech.

The outside borders and the lawn clumps are beautiful with flowering shrubs. No season is like "Lilac-tide," as it has been quaintly called, in this respect. Besides the Lilac itself, there are the long plumes of the white Broom, the brilliant scarlet of the hybrid Rhododendrons, the delicious blossoms, both pink and yellow, of the Azaleas, the golden showers of the Laburnum, and others too numerous to mention. A Judas-tree at an angle of the house is in bud. The Général Jacqueminot between the vineries has given us a Rose already.

The cuckoo has been calling for days past among the trees beyond the orchard, and the song birds seem to be awake half through the night.

The foliage of the large forest-trees is particularly fine this year. The Horse Chestnuts were the first in leaf, and each branch is now holding up its light of waxen blossom. The Elms came next, the Limes, the Beeches, and then the Oaks. Yet still

> "the tender Ash delays
> To clothe herself when all the woods are green,"

and is all bare as in mid-winter. This, however, if the adage about the Oak and the Ash be true, should be prophetic of a fine hot summer.

*May* 21.—I wonder if any effect of bedding out is finer than that which my mixed borders have now to show. They are at their very best, for it is the reign of the Pæony and the Iris. Great clumps of each, the one bowed down with the weight of its huge crimson globes, the other springing up erect with its purple-headed shafts, appear at intervals along the borders, and each lends a fresh grace to the form and colour of the other.

Among other flowers in rare beauty just now are (as once in the garden of "the Sensitive Plant,")

> "Narcissi, the fairest among them all,
> Who gaze on their eyes in the stream's recess
> Till they die of their own dear loveliness."

Was it, I wonder, owing to this story of Narcissus, and as an emblem of self-seeking, that the Greeks twined the white stars of this flower among the tangled locks of the Eumenides?

The Snowflakes have been flowering abundantly, but they are now passing. The Greek name for the Snowflake is the Leucoion—literally the white Violet—and I think it possible that in a passage of Ovid, where he speaks of the Violet, the Poppy, and the Lily being broken by a storm, he is really thinking of the Snowflake. I am satisfied, as I have already said, that the *Iris* is never (as Lord Stanhope asserted) called the Violet.

My Auriculas are not as good as they should be in a Lancashire garden, for of all flowers it is the old Lancashire favourite. It is still known as the Basier (a corruption, no doubt, of Bear's Ear), and a pretty Lancashire ballad ends every verse with the refrain,

"For the Basiers are sweet in the morning of May."

The old-fashioned Columbine is in full bloom, as is also the Aquilegia glandulosa. I have planted the Aquilegia cœrulea, but both the plant and some seeds which I have sown have failed me, and I half fear I may never be successful with this finest of the Columbines. Before I leave the Columbine, let me mention a mistake in one of Jean Ingelow's very prettiest poems, which her *literary* critics seem never to have detected. She says—

> "O Columbine, open your folded wrapper,
> Where two twin turtle-doves dwell."

But she is confusing the Columbine with the Monk's Hood. The doves of the Columbine cluster round the centre like the doves of Pliny's vase. The doves of the Monk's Hood are only seen as you remove the "wrapper," and then the old idea was that they are drawing a "Venus' chariot."

The accidental grouping of plants on a mixed border is often very happy. A week or two back I found growing out of a tuft of Forget-me-not a plant of the Black Fritillary. The blue eyes of the Forget-me-not seemed to be looking up into the hanging bells of the Fritillary, and were a pleasant contrast to the red-brown of its petals. Gerarde's name for the Fritillary was the "Turkie or Ginnie-hen Flower," and the name of the Fritillary was itself derived from the *fritillus* or dice-box, which the common Fritillary was supposed to resemble in its markings.

In the middle of each group of beds, which the grass walk divides, is a circular bed full of American shrubs. Among these shrubs are several rather fine Kalmias. Very often they do not flower at all, or at best bear a bloom only here and there. This year they are laden with blossom, which is now just ready to burst, and I shall have a show of Kalmia flowers such as I have not seen, since two-and-twenty years ago, I wandered among the Kalmia brakes in the forests of Virginia; and the flower is so beautiful—pink outside, and, as Ruskin says, inside "like the beating out of bosses in hollow silver, beaten out apparently in each petal by the stamens instead of a hammer."

Another bed, which will be very effective in a day or two, is a bed of the double Persian Brier, pegged and trained. The festoons of yellow buds are all but out, and will be one mass of sweet and lovely little Roses.

The Nemophila bed has done very well, but we did not plant it as thickly as we should have done, and there are bare places here and there.

I have still to mention the great bushes, or rather trees, of Hawthorn, of which some stand in front of the dining-room windows, while others fling their perfume across the hedge that divides the garden and the croft. There is another Lancashire May song, from which I cannot but quote a few lines, as it is but little known. The Mayers come to the door and sing (or sang, rather, for the custom no longer holds with us) :—

> " We have been rambling all this night,
>    And almost all this day ;
> And now, returned back again,
>    We've brought you a branch of May.
> A branch of May we have brought you,
>    And at your door it stands ;
> It is but a sprout, but it's well budded out,
>    By the work of our Lord's hands."

## VII.

*The Summer Garden—The Buddleia—Ghent Azaleas—The Mixed Borders—Roses—The Green Rose.*

*July* 13.—There is a longer interval than usual since my last notes; but I have been away among the Soldanellas and the Gentians of Switzerland, and I have had to leave my garden to the gardener's care. Now that I have returned, I find how much has gone on, and how much I must have missed. The Nemophila bed, I hear, gradually filled up and became a perfect sheet of brilliant blue. The Anemone bed was very good, and that of Ranunculus very fair; but best of all, as I knew it would be, was the bed of Brier Roses, with their trained branches laden with sweet little yellow blossoms.

The Kalmias too are over, and the alpine Rhododendrons (Roses des Alpes) are also nearly at an end; but I have just found them wild upon the Wengern Alp, and that must be my consolation. There is nothing I am more sorry to have missed than the great shrub—almost tree—of Buddleia globosa, which grows in the centre of one of the herbaceous borders. It has been, as it always is, covered with its golden balls, smelling of honey, and recalling an old garden in Somersetshire which I knew years ago. It is certainly true that nothing calls up associations of the past as does the sense of smell. A whiff of perfume stealing through the air, or entering into an open window, and one is reminded of some far-off place on some long-past day when the same perfume floated along, and for one single moment the past will seem more real than the present. The Buddleia, the Magnolia, and one or two other flowers always have this power over me.

I have still one Azalea, and only one, in blossom; it has a small and very fragrant white flower.

I have been lately reading several articles about the fly-catching flowers. Is it generally known that no fly-catcher is more cruel and more greedy than the common Ghent Azalea, especially, I think, the large sweet yellow one? On one single blossom, which I gathered just before leaving home, at the end of May, I found no less than six flies; four of them were quite dead, and of one or two nothing remained but a shred of wing. Two others were still alive, but the Azalea had already nearly drained their life away, and held them so tightly with its viscid hairs that I could hardly release them from its grasp. On the other blossoms in the truss were other flies, three, four, or five; so that the entire Azalea shrub had probably caught some hundreds.[1]

The mixed borders are almost past their best,—at least the hairy red Poppy, the day Lily, and the early purple Gladiolus are over, and, of course, the Irises and Pæonies. At present various Canterbury Bells, Valerian (which I saw bedded out the other day at Liége), and the white and orange Lily, are the gayest things we have. There is a Mullein, too, which is well worth a corner in any garden. Not long since I saw, in some book of rambles through our southern counties, the spire of a cathedral with its pinnacles and crockets compared to a spike of Mullein flower. It is certainly the Mullein (the distinctive name of which I do not know) which is now in bloom with me; and, indeed, the resemblance had occurred to me before I had read the book.

But I hardly care to linger over other flowers,

---

[1] See note II. on the Azalea viscosa.

when the Rose-beds are in their fullest splendour. The summer Roses must have been better a fortnight back, but the perpetuals are as good as can be, and many of the summer Roses yet remain. I sometimes fear that the passion for large, well-formed blossoms, and the desire of novelty, will make some of the dear old Roses of our childhood pass into entire neglect; yet, when we think of a Rose, of which any poet has written, it will not be La France, or Sénateur Vaisse, or Alfred Colomb—beautiful as they are. When Herrick warns us—

> "Gather ye Rosebuds while ye may,"

or when Hood tells us—

> "It was the month of Roses,
> We plucked them as we passed,"

—their Roses were other than the favourite Roses of to-day. Perhaps they were the old Cabbage Rose, a great bush of which grows next to a bed of Lavender, and pleasantly scents the garden as you enter it. Perhaps they were the Portland Rose, of which I have some three beds, and than which no Rose is better for the making of Pot Pourri, as the young ladies in Mr. Leslie's picture may learn to their advantage. Perhaps they were the Moss Rose, with its mossed buds and fragrant blossoms, of which I have another bed entirely for itself. Perhaps they were the Maiden Blush, or the York and Lancaster, or the sweet old China, with its pink shell petals, which comes so soon and lingers on so late—the last Rose, not of summer but of autumn.[1] Then there are other old Roses which should not be neglected. The Rose Unique, which is a white Cabbage Rose, is one ; the Rose Celeste, the thin delicate buds of which are so beautiful, is another. Then there is the little Rose de Meaux, and the old Damask, which indeed seems to have nearly disappeared.

It must have been one of these Roses, be sure, and not a Tea or a perpetual, which Lady Corisande finds in her garden for Lothair.

Not of course that we are not grateful for the new Roses, with their brilliant colouring and their perfect form, but we are unwilling that the old should be forgotten. The Gloire de Dijon and Général Jaqueminot seem to me the most vigorous and most useful, if not the finest; but I have two old standards which are at the moment more

---

[1] It is mentioned in the *Baroness Bunsen's Life* how Mrs. Delany loved to fill her china bowls with the pink buds of the Monthly Rose, surrounded by sea-green shoots of the young Lavender.

effective than anything I have. One is Boule de Nantes, the other an old summer Rose, the name of which I do not know, but which, when fully out, much resembles the Comtesse de Jaucourt. They are not trained in any way, and I find, measuring round their heads, that one has a circumference of 12 feet, and the other of 12½ feet. In the South of England it is no doubt different, but for us these are large dimensions; and certainly nothing I now get from the nursery gardens seems inclined to attain to half the size.

There is one Rose in my garden which flourishes abundantly, but which is the only Rose, of which I should decline to give a cutting. It is so ugly that it is worth nothing, except as a curiosity; and if it ceased to be a curiosity it would be quite valueless. It is a *green* Rose. I got a small plant from Baltimore, in America, some years ago, and I find it perfectly hardy. It flowers very freely, and all through the summer; the bud is a perfect Rose bud in appearance, but the open flower shows that the Rose is of monstrous and not natural growth; the petals are, it seems to me, no real petals at all, but an expansion of the green heart, which often appears in Roses, and which has here been so cultivated as to take the place of the natural Rose.

These petals are coarse and irregular, and have serrated edges, with a very faint scent.[1]

How the Rose twines itself around all history and all literature! There are the Rose gardens of Persia, and the loves of the Rose and nightingale; there are those famous Roses once plucked in the Temple Garden, of which "the pale and bloody petals" (to use a fine expression of Hawthorne's) were strewed over many an English battle-field; there is the golden Rose which the Pope gives as the best of gifts to the foremost among Catholic monarchs—emblem at once of a fading earthly life, and of the unfading life in heaven.

Of English poets is there one, who does not celebrate the Rose, and of all is there one, who draws from it a more tender morality than Waller in "Go, lovely Rose"?

But no nation ever loved the Rose as did the Greeks, and it was *their* legend that told us how the Rose sprang to birth. Bion's "Lament for

---

[1] Mr. Buist, of the Rosedale Nurseries, Philadelphia, has since written to the *Gardeners' Chronicle* on the origin of the Green Rose:—"There appears to be some uncertainty in regard to the origin of this Rose. It is a sport from Rosa Indica (the China Rose of England and Daily Rose of America). It was caught in Charleston, S.C., about 1833, and came to Baltimore through Mr. R. Halliday, from whom I obtained it, and presented two plants to my old friend, Thomas Rivers, in 1837."

Adonis" has been translated by Mrs. Browning, and I know no translation equal to it in general fidelity and vigour of expression. It appears to me, on the whole, perhaps the very best translation in the language. Here are the lines which tell this part of the story :—

> " Ah, ah, Cytherea! Adonis is dead ;
> She wept tear after tear with the blood which was shed,
> And both turned into flowers for the earth's garden close.—
> Her tears to the Windflower, his blood to the Rose."

Another still more famous Greek poem about the Rose is one by Sappho, which Mrs. Browning has also most beautifully translated—a fit task, which unites the names of the two great poetesses of Greece and England. The poem begins :—

> " If Zeus chose us a king of the flowers in his mirth,
> He would call to the Rose and would royally crown it :
> For the Rose, ho! the Rose, is the grace of the earth ;
> Is the light of the plants that are growing upon it."

No wonder the Greeks wove their wreaths of the Rose, or that "under the Rose" they passed many a gay and happy hour, to be kept in memory, if untold in words.

My bedding-out is of course finished, but of this I must speak on the next occasion. The weather has been hot, and rain will now be welcome.

## VIII.

*The Fruit Crop—Hautbois Strawberries—Lilium Auratum—Sweet Williams—Carnations—The Bedding-out.*

*August* 15.—It is, I find, a dangerous thing to leave a garden masterless for even a month. The best of gardens will probably fall short in some respect, and I certainly discover several matters which would have been otherwise had I remained at home. My readers will hardly be interested by the details of my grievances; it is pleasanter to tell where we have been successful.

The wall fruit, however, I must mention. The ants and the aphis, and possibly some frost, have destroyed the Peach crop utterly. There is not a single Peach, and the Nectarines, which are certainly a hardier fruit with us, only number thirty in all! The Apricots have done fairly, and were so early that we gathered three or four in the last days of July—a full month before their usual time. The Moorpark Apricot, which we owe to Sir

William Temple, is still the best. By the way, he tells us that the Roman name for Apricots is Mala epirotica. Is this the root of the word Apricot, or may we still look upon it as from "apricus," the "sunny fruit,"—the fruit that loves the sun and has caught its own bright colour?[1]

Of the smaller fruit Cherries have been a failure, with the exception indeed of the Morellos. Gooseberries have done well, though I fear I cannot compete with the giant Gooseberries of a Lancashire Gooseberry show. The Currants, whether against the wall or on bushes, have been capital, and the black Currants would take a prize at any show. We now net up some Currant bushes for the later autumn. The Raspberries, which we train in arches, have done tolerably, and we should have a second crop of the white ones in October.

The Strawberries have been an average crop, and the little Alpines have been capital—so large, so highly flavoured, and so redolent of Switzerland!

I am trying, too, for the first time, to grow Hautbois Strawberries, which are almost unknown with us. We are as yet not very successful, and I well know how capricious a fruit it is as regards

---

[1] I believe, as a matter of fact, that the more received derivation of Apricot is "præcox."

setting. A year or two ago I was breakfasting with a well-known and most courtly physician in London, who is since dead. A dish of beautiful Hautbois was on the table. We were all admiring. "Yes," said our host, "they are now getting very rare. Sometimes a patient says to me, 'May I not have a little fruit?' 'Certainly not!' is my answer. 'Surely a few Strawberries?' Then, that I may not seem a great curmudgeon, I say, 'Well, a few Strawberries, but be sure they are Hautbois;' *and I know they can't get them!*" To ordinary Strawberries a Hautbois is what a Tea Rose is to ordinary Roses; it has an aroma all its own, and unlike all others.

In the flower garden the finest bed is one which I have now had for the last three years. It is a bed of Lilium auratum, with the dark Heliotrope growing in between. I take up the Lily bulbs for the winter, bring them on in heat, and then plant them out. They are really beautiful, and each year they seem more vigorous. Some have four blossoms, some have six or eight, and one has as many as ten. The strong perfume lies heavy on that end of the garden, and I think this Lily should never be brought inside the house. It is curious how the blossoms vary; in some the golden stripes are so much deeper, in some the dark claret spots are so much more numerous.

Another bed is of Lilium speciosum, planted to take the place of a bed of Sweet William, which was quite a glow of colour in the earlier part of the summer. This dear old Sweet William, which was the favourite in the old cottage gardens, and which, with the Lad's-love and the Pink, was the chosen flower for the buttonhole of the country boy, is now far too much neglected. Its rich velvet clusters of twenty different shades make a bed of exquisite beauty. It is over too soon, but it can be *supplanted* (may I say ?) by something else. In a second bed of Sweet Williams I placed Gladiolus bulbs, and now they are coming into flower from out the green cushion, from which we have cut the withered blossoms.

A bed of the sweet little pink Pinks has of course been over some time, and though the bed is now quite bare of bloom—for I cannot disturb the roots—it is well worth sacrificing some colour in autumn for the three summer weeks of delicious perfume. Clusters of white Pinks have been no less sweet on the herbaceous borders, and now the Clove Carnations take their place.

It is curious that so familiar a flower as the Pink

should be scarcely mentioned by the great poets. Shakspeare only just names it, and I do not think Marvell does. Milton, in his *Lycidas*, barely alludes to "the white Pink," and Cowley has no separate poem in its praise. Indeed, one may say generally that, with the exception of the Rose, the flowers in which the poets have rejoiced, and which they have immortalised, are the flowers of spring. Cowley, who wrote as a horticulturist, is the almost solitary exception. There is, however, a rather pretty and fanciful little song of Herrick's " To Carnations :"—

> "Stay while ye will, or goe;
> And leave no scent behind ye :
> Yet trust me, I shall know
> The place where I may find ye :
> Within my Lucia's cheek,
> Whose livery ye weare,
> Play ye at hide or seek,
> I'm sure to find ye there."

For the ordinary bedding-out of ordinary gardens I have a real contempt. It is at once gaudy and monotonous. A garden is left bare for eight months in the year, that for the four hottest months there shall be a blaze of the hottest colour. The same combinations of the same flowers appear wherever you go. Calceolarias, Verbenas, and Zonal Pelargoniums, with a border of Pyrethrum or Cerastium—and that is about all. There is no thought and no imagination. The "bedding-stuff" is got together and planted out, and each year of planting is a repetition of the year before; and thus, as Forbes Watson says so truly, "Gardeners are teaching us to think too little about the plants individually, and to look at them chiefly as an assemblage of beautiful colours. It is difficult in those blooming masses to separate one from another; all produce so much the same sort of impression. The consequence is, people see the flowers on our beds without caring to know anything about them, or even to ask their names." Any interest in the separate plants is impossible, and then they are, almost without exception, scentless plants, to which no association attaches, and which are cared for merely because they give a line or patch of red or yellow to the garden. "The lust of the eye and the pride of life,"—there is little purer pleasure to be drawn from "bedding stuff" than those words convey. However, there is already a reaction setting in, and the use of Echeverias and the like gives evidence at least of a more refined taste in colour, though in themselves nothing can be less interesting. Meanwhile, as some bedded-out beds will always be necessary, we may try to diversify them as much as possible. The following are among my most successful :—A bed of Agapanthus, with its beautiful foliage and sky-blue umbels, is surrounded with bright yellow Peacock Gazania ; a bed of scarlet Lobelia cardinalis (is this the "Cardinal Flower" that American writers speak of?) is edged with the white Ribbon-grass, and that again with the blue Lobelia speciosa ; and a second bed of the same Lobelia cardinalis, the bronze foliage of which harmonises so well with the spikes of glowing red, has the Lobelia speciosa next to it, and the Golden Pyrethrum as a border. Another bed is of Humea elegans, edged with the white variegated-leaved Miss Kingsbury Pelargonium, and that again with the blue Lobelia. Into other beds I have introduced the variegated Aloe and the Aralia, as centres for the more dwarf and brightly-coloured Verbenas.

Of the variegated Pelargoniums I find the Beauty of Calderdale the most effective and most vigorous, and though I am told "Mrs. Pollock has a most excellent constitution," she does less well with me. One other bed, which is now over, has been too pretty for me not to mention ; it was a bed of Antirrhinums of all colours, and I shall certainly repeat it another year. Lastly, I have a large bed of Clematis Jackmanni in full glory. Last year it did fairly well, but the plants were comparatively weak, and the flowers trailed upon the ground. This year the plants have grown vigorously, and I have trained Withies all across the bed, so that the purple blossoms twine and cling around them, and are now a perfect mass of blossom.

On the house a Clematis lanuginosa, with its large discs of lilac-grey, is also very handsome, and seems to be doing as well as possible.

In the outer garden a great cluster of yellow Broom has made the border near the front door aglow with golden light; and in the vinery a beautiful Clethra arborea—The Lily of the Valley Tree—has been laden with bunches of its delicate and delicately-scented flowers.

The weather has broken completely during the last fortnight, and it is now too much, and not too little rain, of which we are complaining.

## IX.

Weeds—Tomatos—Tritomas—Night-scented Flowers—Tuberoses—Magnolia—Asters—Indian Corn.

*September* 4.—" The rain it raineth every day." It finds its way through the old timbers of my first vinery, and the Grapes have to be cut out by dozens. It drenches the Pelargoniums and Verbenas, till their blossoms are half washed away. It soaks the petals of the great Lilies, and turns them into a sickly brown. The slugs, I suppose, like it, for they crawl out from the thick Box hedges and do all the harm they can. Weeds, too, of every kind flourish luxuriantly, and we find it no easy work to keep ahead of them. The author of *My Summer in a Garden*—the most humorous little book about gardening ever written—never had such trouble with " pusley " (what is " pusley " ?) as I have with Groundsel. I have enough to feed all the canary birds in the parish. Then, besides the more ordinary and vulgar weeds, I have two varieties of Willow-herb, which have seeded themselves all over the borders, and are for ever appearing where I had fondly imagined they had been utterly uprooted. A yellow Oxalis, too, has turned into a nuisance, and spreads where it was never wanted. Meanwhile the summer fruits are over. The few Nectarines we had have been gathered, and most of the Figs. The Apple-room begins to fill with Keswick Codlings for cooking purposes, and Franklin's Golden Pippin for dessert. As yet none of our Pears are ripe. The Mulberry tree in the orchard drops its fruit before it is mature, but it is rather too much shaded with the orchard trees, and, were it otherwise, there has been but little sun to get to it. We use the Mulberries, however, for tarts and for Mulberry ice, which I can thoroughly recommend. The Tomatos are reddening in numbers along the garden walls. We grow two sorts, Keye's Prolific and the Orangefield Dwarf, and I hardly know which is best. Formerly the Tomato was known as the Pomum amoris, or Love-apple, and was apparently grown only as a garden ornament, and not for use.[1] Cowley mentions it in his "Flora," with the Foxglove and the Canna. Gerarde says of it, "In Spaine and those hot regions they use to eate the

---

[1] See Note III. on the "Solanum" tribe.

Apples prepared and boiled with pepper, salt, and oil; but they yeelde very little nourishment to the bodie, and the same naught and corrupt." Nor does Batty Langley, writing in 1728, mention Tomatos, though he gives long lists of " raw sallets," which include Nasturtium blossoms, Tarragon, Borage flowers, and Sorrel.

The handsomest of our beds at present (except always the beds of Jackman's Clematis and scarlet Lobelia) is a permanent bed of Tritomas, which hold up their orange and crimson maces thickly as possible. These Tritomas would, however, show to most advantage if planted with the Arundo conspicua, the white plumes of which form the happiest contrast to their glowing spikes. The Pampas-grass would be better still, but I have not been able to make them blossom together. A patch of Tritomas on the corner of the lawn has been a failure, owing to the carelessness of a gardener, who cut them down with the grass in mowing.

One other bed, also a permanent one, I have still to mention. It is a mass of Anemone japonica[1]

---

[1] Why is this Anemone called *japonica?* It was first brought from *Simla* by Lady Amherst (the wife of the Governor-General of India), as her granddaughter assures me.

alba with Statice latifolia round it. This Anemone, with its white blossoms surrounding a yellow centre, and looking just like some very perfect white wild Rose, is a beautiful flower, and the grey branched sprays of the Statice harmonise wonderfully with it.

All along the vinery border has been a long row of Stocks, Asters, and Mignonette, and the scent has been delicious, especially towards evening, or after a warm shower of rain. In hot weather the garden is almost too hot when the sun is full upon it, and I have always taken care to grow the night-scented Stock and other flowers of the kind, so that the garden, as evening comes on, may be as sweet as can be; but this year these annuals, with several others, have done no good. On the other hand, the large tall Œnothera opens hundreds of yellow stars each night; and, better still, the beautiful Œnothera taraxacifolia, on the herbaceous borders, unfolds a number of its large white blossoms, which gleam out among the rich green foliage close upon the ground. Next year I think I will have an entire bed of this white Œnothera ; it will be worth the space.

## THE TUBEROSE. 71

The Dahlias have been good with me this year, but I have done badly in Hollyhocks. The Tobacco-plants, which I generally grow, and which were last year so handsome, have also failed me; and so have the Ice-Plants, the Egg-plants, and the Amaranthus salicifolius, nor do I see any sufficient reason for it.

The Tuberose, the flower which, even in the perfect garden of the "Sensitive Plant," was said to be

"The sweetest flower for scent that grows,"

has been very sweet with us. But we dare not leave it in our garden; we bring the pots, with their tall green wands tipped with delicious tufts of bloom, into the centre hall, and the warm perfume rises up the staircase, and floats along the open gallery above.

*September* 19.—I have just gathered from the wall between the vineries the finest blossom I ever happen to have seen of what I maintain is the finest flower in the world—the Magnolia grandiflora—so large and round is it, of such a rich cream colour, and with such a rich strong scent. The Tuberose even seems a plebeian flower by the side of the Magnolia. Once only have I seen this Magnolia growing upon a lawn as a standard, and I never saw any flowering tree so grand, as its dark green leaves lifted up the large white chalices to catch the freshest dews from heaven. But what must it be where this beautiful tree grows wild, as on the

"Hills with high Magnolia overgrown,"

where Gertrude of Wyoming was used to wander?

And, as I gather this Magnolia, the feeling comes across me that now the year is over as regards the garden. We may have another month of flowers, but they are the flowers that linger on, not the flowers that open out new pleasures for us; the Michaelmas Daisy alone remains,—for "the Michaelmas Daisy blows lonely and late,"—before we reach the Chrysanthemums and winter. We have now had all that summer and autumn had to give us, and it seems as though Nature had exhausted all her energies, and were ready for a long rest. The Fuchsias, that come up year by year, are still in great beauty. The Jasmine, with variegated leaves, that clings round an old brick pedestal in the middle of a Kalmia bed, still opens its white blossoms. The Escallonia, that grows up the house, will hang its red flowers in front of the library windows for a fortnight still to come. But the year is virtually at an end, and we talk only of the bulbs for the spring, or of the moving of shrubs in the early winter.

Yet I find two things, of which I have still to speak. The Asters have been good. I had planted them in among the standard Rose beds, and very gay they are. Many years have passed since I found the wild Aster of America growing on the hill-side at Concord behind Hawthorne's house, and was reminded of Emerson's lines—

> "Chide me not, laborious band,
> For the idle flowers I brought;
> Every Aster in my hand
> Goes home loaded with a thought."

Then, by the side of the vinery, is growing a little row of Indian Corn. The plants stand each from 9 to 11 feet high, and each bears its flowering plume above, and its tasselled ears below. There are two varieties, one yellow and one red. I brought them on in heat, and planted them out when they were about a foot in height. This year, as for three years past, they have ripened with me, and on one plant, strangely enough, a piece of the flower has itself fructified! I am not botanist enough to understand how this has happened.[1]

---

[1] The editor of the *Gardeners' Chronicle* explains—"It is simply an admixture of the seed-bearing flowers with the pollen-forming flowers—a not very uncommon event, though ordinarily the male and female blossoms are borne in distinct spikes or panicles." The effect is certainly very curious.

## X.

St. Luke's Summer—The Orchard—The Barberry—White Haricot Beans—Transplanting—The Rockery.

*October* 15.—This is St. Luke's summer, or the "Indian summer" as it is called in America. The air is soft and warm and still. The yellow leaves fall from the Beeches in countless numbers, but slowly and noiselessly, and as if reluctant to let go their hold. The rooks come back to us again across the fields, and clamour among the empty nests, which were their homes in spring. The "remontant" Roses are putting out their latest blooms, and the Antirrhinums, Mulleins, and some few other flowers, show themselves "remontant" also. There is an aromatic fragrance everywhere from the withering leaves and from the lingering flowers.

But there is sadness with it all. We cannot deceive ourselves, but we know that all is now over, and that at any moment the frost may come, and leave us nothing but decay and death.

There are some lines in Morris's *Earthly Paradise*—the very best lines, I think, in the whole poem—which speak of some old men's last peaceful days, as

> "—like those days of later autumn-tide,
> When he who in some town may chance to bide
> Opens the window for the balmy air,
> And, seeing the golden hazy sky so fair,
> And from some city garden hearing still
> The wheeling rooks the air with music fill—
> Sweet, hopeful music—thinketh, Is this spring?
> Surely the year can scarce be perishing.
> But then he leaves the clamour of the town,
> And sees the withered scanty leaves fall down;
> The half-ploughed field, the flowerless garden plot;
> The full dark stream, by summer long forgot;
> The tangled hedges where, relaxed and dead,
> The twining plants their withered berries shed,
> And feels therewith the treachery of the sun,
> And knows the pleasant time is well-nigh done."

Was picture ever more truly painted?—and any day it may be true for us.

Our Apple harvest has been over for nearly a fortnight; but how pleasant the orchard was while it lasted, and how pleasant the seat in the corner by the Limes, whence we see the distant spire on the green wooded slopes. The grey, gnarled old Apple-trees have, for the most part, done well. The Ribston Pippins are especially fine, and so is an apple, which we believe to be the King of the

Pippins. On the other hand, we have some poor and worthless sorts—probably local varieties,—which no pomologist, however able and obliging, would undertake to name. One of the prettiest of Apples—and one of the best, too—is the Delaware. It has an orange-red colour, and reminds one almost of an Orange as it hangs upon the tree. It has a crisp, delicious flavour, but requires to be eaten as soon as it is ripe, for otherwise it soon gets mealy. Indeed all eating apples, with but few exceptions, are best when freshly gathered, or, better still, when, on some clear soft day, they have just fallen on the grass, and lie there, warmed by the rays of the autumn sun.

Of my Pears I have not much to say : the new trees I have planted have hardly come into bearing, and the old ones are of inferior quality. In another year or two, however, I shall hope to be supplied through all the winter months up to the middle of the spring. Plums have done but little, and Damsons, which are supposed to succeed so well in Lancashire, are an absolute failure. I must not forget the Red Siberian Crab, which has been laden with fruit, and one tree of which should find its corner in every garden. Last of all, I have to speak of the Barberry. There is a great bush which stands by the grass walk in the walled garden. In the summer it was a mass of scented yellow blossoms, round which bees were always buzzing. Then, as the year grew older, bunches of bright coral hung over it from top to bottom. We consider our Barberries as not the least important of our fruit crop. We preserve them, some in bunches, some picked like Currants. We crystallize them in sugar, and they become delicious *bonbons*. We steep them in salt and water, and they keep as a gay garnish for cold meat or game. Our Barberry-tree is not looking its best at present; a big branch has withered, and I must cut it in.

*October* 24.—Since I wrote we have had a great gale, which has swept over us, and torn down an Elm in the wood and a fine Chestnut in the croft I could ill spare either of them, and it is but poor comfort to think that our piled-up logs will outlast the winter. It was the "wild west wind," of which Shelley sings, which has done the mischief; and smaller branches, lying scattered all over the lawn and walks, show us where it passed.

We are now preparing our Mushroom bed, for we shall need it as the green vegetables fail us.

I have said but little about the kitchen garden, for I do not suppose it differs much from that of other people. Our Peas have, however, served us particularly well, and we had our last dish on October 1—later than I ever before have known them here. One excellent vegetable I have generally grown, and I would thoroughly recommend it to any one who has space to spare: it is the French White Haricot. It is not often seen with us though it is so very common in France. It is a species of French Bean, of which you eat the white bean itself instead of slicing up the pod. I suspect that, taking England through, there are very few gardens where the White Haricot is found.

We are now busy with our planting. Some Rhododendrons and Aucubas in the borders near the front gate have been pining away—starved by the Elm-tree roots around them. We are trenching up the ground, cutting away what smaller roots we can, and putting in manure and some new shrubs. We are planting a row of Hollies to screen a wall towards the lane. We are moving a Salisburia adiantifolia, with its strange foliage like a gigantic Maidenhair Fern, from a corner into a more prominent place. We shall then set to work to re-arrange the rockery. This, I think,

I have never mentioned. In the middle of the little wood was once a pond, but I found the stagnant water and the soaking leaves, which fell and rotted there, no advantage to the place; I therefore drained away the water and planted beds of Azaleas and Rhododendrons along the slopes, with Primroses, Violets, and Blue Bells, and in the middle of all I have lately placed a tuft of Pampas-grass. On one slope I have managed a rockery with a stone tank in the centre, where for three summers past has flowered an Aponogeton distachyon. I have means of turning on fresh water into the tank, and I am well repaid for any trouble, as the little white boat-blossoms, laden with delicious spicy scent, rise up to the surface of their tiny lake. The rockery is, however, too much under the shade and drip of trees, and I cannot hope that delicate alpine flowers should grow there. Sedums and Saxifragas, Aquilegias, Aubrietias, the white Arabis, and the yellow Moneywort, besides Ferns of various kinds, all do well. In another part of the wood is a loggery, which I have entirely covered with the large white Bindweed, which rambles about at its own will, and opens its blossoms, sometimes a dozen at a time, all through the summer months. Past that, there is a little patch of Bluebells, then more beds of Rhododendrons, and then a short walk, which takes us by a private path to the village church, and then by another branch returns again towards the house. In this part of the grounds there is still room for planting, and I shall probably try some Tree Rhododendrons. A standard Honeysuckle, which I have endeavoured to grow, has done no good as yet; its shoots get nipped by the northeast winds, but I do not yet despair. The most useful undergrowth I find is the Elder; it thrives wonderfully, and is covered with blossom and with berry. One variety, the Parsley-leaved Elder, is here equally hardy with the common Elder, and much more graceful in its growth.

We have now to take in our tender and half-hardy plants, for fear of a sudden frost. The large Myrtles, which have stood out in their boxes, must be placed in safety, and the Lobelia cardinalis and other bedding-plants, which we may need next year, must be removed.

## XI.

*The Wood and the Withered Leaves—Statues—Sun-dials—The Snow—Plans for the Spring—Conclusion.*

*November 7.*—The soft autumn weather still spares what flowers the rains have left us, and here and there are signs as if of another spring. Violets along the grass walks, Strawberries in flower, and to-day a little yellow Brier Rose blossoming on an almost leafless spray, remind us of the early months of the year that is no more. But here, too, are some of the flowers of November. The Arbutus has again opened its bunches of waxen pink, and the Chrysanthemums are again blooming on the shrubbery beds. The year has all but completed its circle since first I wrote these notes, and I speak to-day of the flowers, the same, yet not the same, as those of which I wrote eleven months ago.

The trees have lost nearly every leaf, and our

little wood is bare as the wood wherein poor Millevoye, so soon to die, once strolled when

> "De la dépouille de nos bois
> L'automne avait jonché la terre ;
> Le bocage était sans mystère
> Le rossignol était sans voix."

> "The autumn's leafy spoil lay strewn
> The forest paths along ;
> The wood had lost its haunted shade,
> The nightingale his song."

Had there been in happier days a "mystère" beyond the charm of waving branches and whispering leaves?

Another French poem on a withered leaf is better known, for it was Macaulay who translated Arnault's verses, and rendered the last three lines so perfectly :—

> "Je vais où va toute chose,
> Où va la feuille de Rose,
> Et la feuille de Laurier."

> "Thither go I, whither goes
> Glory's laurel, Beauty's rose."

Among my ideas—I cannot call it plan, for my mind is not quite made up about it—I half fancy putting up a statue of some sort in a nook in the little wood, where the Beeches grow the tallest and the Elders are the thickest. Such things were once common, and then they got so common, and often so out of place, that they became absurd. Every villa garden had its statue and its rockery.

Batty Langley has an amusing chapter about statues. He says—" Nothing adds so much to the beauty and grandeur of gardens as fine statues, and nothing is more disagreeable than when they are wrongly placed ; as Neptune on a terrace walk, mound, &c. ; or Pan, the god of sheep, in a large basin, canal, or fountain ;" and then, " to prevent such absurdities," he gives the most elaborate directions. Mars and Jupiter, Fame and Venus, Muses and Fates, Atlas, Hercules, and many more, are for open centres or lawns. Sylvanus, Actæon, and Echo, are among those recommended for woods. Neptune, Oceanus, and the Naiades, will do for canals and fish-ponds. Pomona and the Hesperides for orchards, Flora and Runcina ("the goddess of weeding") for flower-gardens, Bacchus for vineyards, Æolus for high terrace walks, and "the goddess Vallonta" for valleys. He gives the right deities for paddocks, for wheat-fields, for "ambuscados," and for bechives. In short there is no place for which he does not think a statue ornamental and appropriate. I hope he would approve of my own very humble idea, which is a statue of Hyacinthus,—for, where I thought of placing it, the wild Hyacinths or Bluebells will come clustering up, and make the grass all blue. The poetry of gardens is so entirely neglected in these days of "bedding stuff," that it is well to do anything that can properly be done, without extravagance of taste or method, to revive it.

In the inner garden I think also of placing a sun-dial, which would be in good keeping with the rather formal character of the beds. Mrs. Gatty's beautiful book on sun-dials should help me to a motto. They are of two sorts—the mottoes that warn, and the mottoes that console. "The night cometh,"[1] or "Pereunt et imputantur," are good examples of the one; "Horas non numero nisi serenas," or "Post tenebras lucem spero," are the best instances of the other. But there is a verse by Mrs. Browning, which (if I may so adapt it by a slight alteration in the second line) would make a finer inscription still—

> "See, the shadow on the dial,
> In the lot of every one,
> Marks the passing of the trial,
> Proves the presence of the sun."

---

[1] Many years ago Miss Martineau told me of this motto, and I see that in her "Autobiography" she speaks of it as "perfect in its way." She however finally adopted for her own sun-dial the happier "Come, light! visit me!"

*Nov.* 28.—We wake to find snow all thick upon the ground, over lawn and flower-bed, and the children are out betimes rolling up huge snowballs on the grass. This snow is the best thing possible for the garden, for we have already had a night or two of sharp frost, which killed all it could reach of our herbaceous plants. "Autumn's last delights were nipped by early cold," as in the garden of Lord Houghton's "Old Manorial Hall," and the Dahlias and the Fuchsias were all shrivelled into brown unsightly tufts. We have covered up the Fig-trees on the wall. We have trenched up the shrubbery borders. We have done our last planting—a Catalpa in one place, a Paulownia in another—and some more fruit-trees in the orchard. We have planted our bulbs and sowed our autumn annuals for spring gardening. I was so pleased with the Nemophila bed of last May that I am repeating the experiment on a larger scale. I shall have one bed of Nemophila, and another of Virginian Stock. I shall have a bed of pink Saponaria edged with white. Along the Vine border I shall stretch a ribbon of white Saponaria, blue Myosotis, pink Silene, and many-coloured Sweet Peas.

Then again, at the end of the grass walk, where it runs up against the hedge of the croft, I am fixing an arched trelliswork of wire, with a wire seat inside, and over it I shall train and trail the broad leaves of the Aristolochia and the scarlet blossoms of the Tropæolum speciosum.

The vineries are of course at rest ; but in them are Roman Hyacinths, now ready for the house, and pots of Polyanthus Narcissus will be also ready within a week.

The porch of the house is filled on either side with stages of Chrysanthemums, and the fine glossy foliage of an Aralia looks well in the inside vestibule.

And now I bring these notes to an end. My aim has been to show how much interest and pleasure may be gathered out of a garden of moderate pretensions, and with no great appliances in the way of glass, nor any advantage in the way of climate.

I have endeavoured, too, to reclaim for our English gardens those old flowers, which Shakespeare and Milton and Marvell and Cowley loved. They have been far too long neglected for flowers, whose only charm is charm of colour and a certain evenness of growth. The ordinary bedded garden of to-day is as inferior to the Elizabethan gardens of old, as all gardens anywhere must be to the delights, which fancy conjures up in the enchanted gardens of Armida, or the bowered pleasance of Boccaccio. Meanwhile we can only do what best we can, and when all else fails we can say, like Candide, "Il faut cultiver *notre* jardin."

And so I bid a hearty farewell to those readers, who for months past have followed the fortunes, and shared with me the hopes, of a year in a Lancashire garden.

## SUPPLEMENTARY CHAPTER.

Flowering Shrubs — Yuccas — Memorial Trees — Ranunculus — Pansies — Canna Indica — Summer Flowers — Bluets — Fruit-blossoms and Bees — Strawberry Leaves — Garden Sounds — Mowing — Birds — The Swallow — Pleasures of a Garden.

ALMOST more interesting than herbaceous plants are the flowering shrubs. Most beautiful of all, if, indeed, it may be called a shrub, is the Buddleia Globosa, in the inner garden, which I have already mentioned. When June draws to its close, it is laden with thousands of blossoms like little golden oranges, and fills the air with honied scent. It is the largest Buddleia I ever happen to have seen, for it stands sixteen feet high, and stretches its branches over a round bed of blue Iris to a circumference of seventy feet.

And just about the time when the Buddleia is in bloom, masses of the sweet homely English Elder, screening off the little wood, will perfume all the approach to the house. Common enough it is, but delightful in its dark foliage, its rich creamy blossoms, its clusters of purple berries. We do not make the use of it we should, and Elderberry water and Elderberry Wine are known to me by name alone, but the berries are excellent for tarts and puddings.

One shrub which I planted a year or two ago has answered far better than I had any right to hope. It is the Desfontainea Spinosa. It is so like a holly that it puzzles everybody who sees, for the first time, the scarlet and yellow tubes of blossom which stand out among the prickly leaves. The year before last it flowered twice with me, but the cruel winter we have just had has cut it sadly, and it will be long before it will recover.

I have spoken of trying whether by the planting of a second Arbutus I could make my beautiful old shrub fruit. The result has been quite successful, and I have had for two years past bright red berries hanging down among the pale waxen blossoms and the dark-green leaves. The Magnolia between the vineries has become prodigal of flowers as it has grown older, and last year I had no less than ten blossoms from it, and it is still young. The Magnolia (also a Grandiflora) on the house has also begun to flower, but I had nearly lost it altogether, and the story is rather a curious one. I had noticed that both it and other creepers were looking unhappy, and I could not guess the reason. The Escallonia showed bare branches in many places, the Ceanothus seemed shrunken and brown, and a Gloire de Dijon Rose did no good. At last it occurred to my gardener that the galvanised wire, which I had put up to avoid driving nails into the stone work of the windows, was to blame. I pulled it all down, coated it thickly over with paint, and, when it was again put up, all the creepers seemed to start into fresh life, and grew strong and vigorous.

On a patch of green grass near the house stands a Yucca Gloriosa, which I am always hoping will flower, but it has never done so yet. Not long ago I was at a stately place in Shropshire, and at the end of a broad walk, where a circle of Yuccas had been planted, there were no less than five in full flower, throwing up pale jets of blossom, like fountains, towards the sky. I never saw anything more perfect in its way. But it is said that the right time to see a Yucca is by moonlight. There is a very striking passage in one of the letters of the most remarkable of American women, Margaret Fuller (afterwards Countess D'Ossoli), in which she says:—

"This flower" (it was the Yucca Filamentosa) "was made for the moon as the Heliotrope is for the sun, and refuses other influences, or to display her beauty in any other light. Many white flowers are far more beautiful by day. The lily, for instance, with its firm thick leaf, needs the broadest light to manifest its purity, but these transparent leaves of greenish white, which look dull in the day, are melted by the moon to glistening silver. . . ." The second evening I went out into the garden again. In clearest moonlight stood my flower, more beautiful than ever. The stalk pierced the air like a spear; all the little bells had erected themselves around it in most graceful array, with petals more transparent than silver, and of softer light than the diamond. Their edges were clearly but not sharply defined—they seemed to have been made by the moon's rays. The leaves, which had looked ragged by day, now seemed fringed by most delicate gossamer, and the plant might claim, with pride, its distinctive epithet of *filamentosa*."

On another grass-plot near I have one of the beautiful Retinosporas of Japan, which was one day planted for me by a friend. He is the poet, who says that—

> "Eastward roll the orbs of heaven,
> Westward tend the thoughts of men:
> Let the Poet, nature-driven,
> Wander Eastward now and then :—"

and this tree, while it lives, will remind me of the East, and of him who wrote these lines.

But there are other pleasant ways of recalling one's friends to memory.

I never stay anywhere, where there is a garden, without bringing back with me some one or more shrubs, as a remembrance of a beautiful place or happy hours; and, when I plant them, I fasten to them a label, mentioning their old home, and thus I am reminded—now of a quaint low house covered with creepers and nestling among the hills of Wales—now of a magnificent castle with its pleasance in the north of Ireland,—now of a great hall in Scotland, where a wild glen runs down past the garden to the woods,—now of an old English abbey, where the flowers of to-day spring up among the ruins of a thousand years ago.

Among the flowers in the inner garden, which have well repaid me during the last year or two, have been the Anemones—delightful old flowers—

"pied wind-flowers," Shelley calls them,—which first sprang to birth when Venus wept Adonis. Then I have had two successful beds of Ranunculus; one was prettily and fancifully mottled; the other was of the finest scarlet,—a scarlet so intense that it seemed to be almost black in the inner shadows of the petals. A gifted American lady once said to me— "Does not black seem to underlie all bright scarlet?" and I have thought of this as I have looked at this bed of Ranunculus, and I think of it often as I see the red coats of our soldiers passing by. I have often noticed, too, that, in an evening, when there is still light enough to see flowers, that are yellow, or blue, or pink, the blossoms of a scarlet Pelargonium give forth no colour, but look as if cut out of some soft black velvet. Another spring bed, from which I had hoped much, has disappointed me. It was a bed of Crown Imperials, but for some reason they flowered irregularly and produced no effect. But the individual flowers of some were magnificent. I had never examined a Crown Imperial properly before, and never knew that its great beauty lay in the little circlet of pearls—nectaries, I suppose they are—which lie at the bottom of each orange bell. They are quite exquisite in their grey and white glittering movement, as the light plays upon them, and are more like pearls than anything else in nature.

Among my humbler flowers, of which I have somehow made no mention, is the Pansy, yet few flowers have more associations connected with them. The Pansy—the *Heartsease* we still sometimes call it—is Shakespeare's "Love in Idleness," and Milton's "Pansy freak'd with jet." The American poet, Edgar Poe, speaks of the "beautiful Puritan Pansies;" and I remember a fine wild passage in one of this same poet's little-known essays, where two angels are talking, and one of them says—"We will swoop outward into the starry meadows beyond Orion, where for Pansies, and Violets, and Heartsease, are the beds of the triplicate and triple-tinted suns."

Last year my finest bed was one of the Canna Indica, in which every plant threw up grand broad leaves and spikes of crimson or yellow blossom. Why is not the Canna far more common in all our gardens? At present one sees it in public parks, or where gardening on a great scale is carried on, but in smaller gardens it is very rare, and yet it is easy enough to grow; and once I think it must have been more known than it is at present. Gerarde speaks of it as "the flowering reed," and gives a very fair illustration of it. He adds, however, "Myself have planted it in my garden divers times, but it never came to flowering or seeding, for that it is very impatient to endure the injury of our cold climate." Cowley, too, speaks of the "lustre of the Indian flowering reed;" and Dr. Darwin, in his *Loves of the Plants*, gives it (with its single pistil and stamen), as the best type of the conjugal fidelity of flowers, and tells how—

> "The tall Canna lifts his curlèd brow,
> Erect to heaven;"

adding, in prose, that "the seeds are used as shot by the Indians, and are strung for prayer-beads in some Catholic countries." Indeed, the plant is often called the "Indian Shot," and as the seeds, shining, hard and black, ripened with me last year, I can undertand how appropriate is the name.

A bed of double Potentillas, some red, some yellow, and some with the two colours mingled, has been very fine; and so has a bed of hybrid Bulbous Begonias, which seem quite hardy. I plant the blue Lobelia between them, and it contrasts pleasantly with their crimson and orange bells. A long row of Sweet Peas of every variety

## NEW BEDS.

of colour extends along the border in front of the vinery, and fills the garden with its scent; and not far off is a wire screen, which I cover with the large Convolvulus, and through the summer months the "Morning Glories," as the blossoms were once called, display all their short-lived beauty.

On either side of the grass-walk, which runs down the garden, at a right angle to the vineries, I am making rustic trellises of logs of wood, round which I shall plant Vegetable Marrows and Gourds, and at intervals clumps of the great Sunflower.[1] In another corner I am sowing a bed of the Bluet, or Corn-flower, the favourite flower of the Emperor of Germany. For some reason the Violets of Napoleon, of which I once had abundance, have not been so successful with me during the last few years,—will the Corn-flower do better?—What a glorious blue it is! and how much we have neglected it! because, I suppose, it is too common, and grows wild amid the ripening Corn and the scarlet Poppy.

Turning to the fruit-garden, my great discovery has been that I *must* have bees—not at all for the honey, but for the proper setting of the fruit. A large May Duke Cherry is always covered with

[1] See Note IV. on the Sunflower of the Classics.

H

blossom, but scarcely anything has ever come from it. Last year I examined its blossom closely, and found that the pistil is so much longer than the stamens that it cannot fertilise itself, and must be dependent on insects. This is not the case with other varieties of Cherries, so far as I can see, and I am curious to find out whether my remedy of a bee-hive will this year have the desired effect. I believe it will be of service to the other wall-fruit too, and I have already seen the affection the bees have for the blossoms of the Apricot.

How beautiful a garden is when all the fruit-trees are in bloom! and how various that bloom is! Each Pear-tree bears a different blossom from its neighbour, and the handsomest of all, in size and shape of flower and form of cluster, is the Jargonelle. But no Pear-blossom can compare with the beauty of blossom on the Apple-trees;— and of all Apple-trees the Pomeroy is most beautiful, when every bough is laden with clusters of deep-red buds, which shade off into the softest rosy white, as, one by one, the blossoms open out.

Of other fruit I have nothing new to notice, unless it be to ask whether any one now living can smell the scent of dying Strawberry leaves? We all remember how Mrs. Gaskell in her delightful story gives Lady Ludlow the power, but now we all seem to have lost it. Certainly my dying Strawberry leaves give me no sense of sweetness. Was it a mere fond and foolish fancy? or were the Strawberries of Elizabethan gardens different from those we are now growing? Bacon tells us that, next to the white double Violet and the Musk Rose, the sweetest perfume in the open air is " Strawberry leaves dying, which yield a most excellent cordiale smell;" and I find in an old play by Sir John Suckling—

> "Wholesome
> As dying leaves of Strawberries."

But there are sounds that haunt a garden hardly less delightful than its sights and scents. What sound has more poetry in it than when in the early morning one hears the strong sharp sweep of the scythe, as it whistles through the falling grass, or the shrill murmur of the blade upon the whetstone; and, in spite of mowing machines, at times one hears the old sound still. How fond Andrew Marvell was of mowing and the mowers! He has given us "Damon the Mower," "The Mower to the Glow-worm," "The Mower's Song," "The Mower against Gardens," and "Ametas and Thestylis making Hay-ropes;" and again, in his fine poem, on "Appleton House," he describes the "tawny mowers" dividing the "grassy deeps,"

"With whistling scythe and elbow strong."

One of our latest poets too, Mr. Allingham, has a delicious little mower's song, with a quite perfect refrain of—

"A scythe-sweep and a scythe-sweep,
We mow the grass together."

And again, what does not the garden owe to the voice of birds; the deep cawing of the rook in its "curious flight" around the elm-trees; the clear note of the cuckoo from the limes that bound the orchard; and, best of all, the rich, full melody of the thrush! The nightingale's song may be sweeter and stronger, but the nightingale only sings in certain places (certainly not with us), and the thrush is everywhere. The nightingale sings later in the night, but the thrush will go on till nine, and begin again at four, and surely that is all we need. Can anything be truer, or better said, than these lines of Browning's about a thrush?—

> "Hark! where my blossomed Pear-tree in the hedge
>   Leans to the field, and scatters on the clover
> Blossoms and dewdrops, at the bent spray's edge—
>   That's the wise thrush—he sings each song twice over,
> Lest you should think he never could recapture
> The first fine careless rapture."

But there is one bird dearer to us than the thrush, and that is the swallow, which for some years past has built its nest in our porch. It has been pretty to mark her skimming round and round with anxious watching, till we have left the place. Prettier still, when we have kept ourselves concealed, to see her darting upwards to the nest, which was fringed by four little heads all in a row, and, going from one to the other, give each its share. We could hear the sharp little cry of satisfaction as each nestling was attended to. How much the poets have written about swallows! There is the charming passage in Longfellow's "Golden Legend," where the old monk is speaking; he is the librarian, whose duty it is to illuminate the missals for the convent's use and pride:—

> "How the swallows twitter under the eaves!
>   There, now there is one in her nest;
>   I can just catch a glimpse of her head and breast,
>   And will sketch her thus in her quiet nook,
>   For the margin of my gospel-book."

Then how delightful is the boast, which Mr. Courthope, in his *Paradise of Birds*, puts into the nightingale's mouth, that a bird is better than a man, for—

> "He never will mount as the swallows,
> Who dashed round his steeples to pair,
> Or hawked the bright flies in the hollows
> Of delicate air."

And, long before this, Banquo had marked their "pendent beds" on Macbeth's castle, and noticed that—

> "Where they most breed and haunt, I have observed
> The air is delicate."

And who does not recall Tennyson's—

> "Swallow, swallow, flying, flying south,"

and bearing on swift wing the message that—

> "Dark and true and tender is the north"?

Or who, that has once read it, can forget *Les Hirondelles* of Béranger, and how the French captive among the Moors questions the swallows about his country, his home, his friends, which they perhaps have seen?

Lastly, what a felicitous line is this of the American poet Lowell, when he describes

> "The thin-winged swallow *skating* on the air."

I must bring these Notes, such as they are, to a close, and yet I feel I have scarcely even yet described the pleasures of a garden. But my memory at least can do it justice. It recalls summer afternoons, when the lawn tennis went merrily on on the lawn, by the weeping ash-tree, and summer evenings, when the house was too hot, and we sat out after dinner upon the terrace with the claret and the fruit. The air was all perfume, and the light lingered long in the east over the church steeple three miles away, and no sound but of our own voices broke the silence and the peace.

Again, there were fine bright autumn days—days when the garden was full of warm scent and warmer colour—days when the children could swing for hours in the hammock, which hangs between two large Sycamores, and have their tea-table beneath the trees,—days when the still air was only stirred by the patter of a falling chestnut, or the note of some solitary bird, or the sound of church bells far away. Beyond the grass-field, which comes nearly up to the house, was a field of wheat, and we could watch the harvesting, and follow with our eyes the loaded waggons as they passed along by the hedge-row trees.

But such recollections grow thicker as I write, and words, such as I at least can command, do them little justice. I cannot really share with my readers these pleasures of the past, though I like to fancy that they may feel some kindly sympathy, as they remember happy days in gardens dear to them as mine to me.

# NOTES.

# NOTES.

## NOTE I.

### ON THE VIOLA OF THE ROMANS.

I contributed the following note on "The Viola of the Romans," to the *Gardeners' Chronicle* of September 26, 1874, as I found a correspondent had been adopting Lord Stanhope's views.

Mr. Ruskin in his *Queen of the Air* wrote, "I suspect that the flower whose name we translate 'Violet' was in truth an Iris" (he is speaking of the Greek *ion*, but the Viola no doubt is whatever the *ion* was).

In Lord Stanhope's *Miscellanies*, second series, which was published in 1872, a paper, which had been previously (in 1830) read before the Society of Antiquaries, treats of the "Viola of the Ancients."

Lord Stanhope identifies it with the Iris, and on the following grounds :—

1. Because when riding through Sicily in the winter of 1825, he saw many Irises and no Violets, and heard that the country people called the Iris Viola.

2. Because Pliny speaks of Violæ luteæ, whereas there are no Violets of that colour.

3. Because Pliny also describes the Violet as growing in sunny and barren places ("apricis et macris locis"), whereas really Violets always grow in the shade.

4. Because he speaks of the Violet as springing from a fleshy root-stock ("ab radice carnoso"), whereas the Violet root is fibrous.

5. Because Ovid couples the Violet with the Poppy and the Lily as flowers which, when broken off, hang their heads to the ground.

I need not say much as to Lord Stanhope's not finding Violets in Sicily in winter, for the question is, whether he would not find them in Italy in spring. Nor does the fact of the Sicilian peasants speaking of the Iris as a Violet disturb me any more than when I hear a Scotch peasant speak of the "Harebell" as a "Bluebell."

The real authority is Pliny, and Pliny settles the question completely. He says (I quote for convenience from Bohn's translated edition):—"Next after the Roses and the Lilies, the Violet is held in the highest esteem. Of this there are several varieties, the purple, the yellow, and the white, all of them reproduced from plants, like the Cabbage. The Purple Violet, which springs up spontaneously in sunny spots with a thin meagre soil, has larger petals than the others, springing immediately from the root, which is of a fleshy substance. This Violet has a name, too, distinct from the other wild kinds, being called 'ion,' and from it the ianthine cloth takes its name."

He goes on to say that of cultivated kinds the Yellow Violet is held in most esteem. He speaks then of the Tusculan and Marine Violet as having broader petals than the others, but being less sweet, while the Calathian Violet is also without scent.

A little farther on he describes the Iris itself, and says "the stem of this plant is a cubit in length and erect, the flower being of various colours like the rainbow, to which circumstance it is indebted for its name." It is, he adds, a plant of a caustic nature, and the root is used in perfumery and medicine, but the flower is *never employed for garlands.*

After this, perhaps, it is needless to add that of course Lord Stanhope is mistaken in supposing that there are no Yellow Violets (he may find any number half-way up the Rigi), or that Violets do not often grow in sunny and sterile places, or that the Purple Violet has not a fleshy root-stock.

That the Sweet Violet, which Pliny says was used for wreath-making, was generally cultivated is certain from Horace's

> "Tum *violaria* et
> Myrtus, et omnis copia narium
> Spargent olivetis odorem."
> *Odes*, ii. 15.

Then, again, the Sweet Violet was used for the flavouring of wine—the "vinum violatum."

There are other passages in which Pliny speaks of the sweetness of the Violet. He says it is sweetest at a distance, and that it has no scent except in the flower itself.

There can be no doubt then whatever (I conceive) that the Greeks, when they spoke of the "ion," or the Romans of the "Viola," generally meant our Violet, and that the Violet-wreaths were made from this familiar flower.

Still the name was perhaps loosely used, and it is highly probable that the flower to which Ovid refers, in the passage which Lord Stanhope quotes, was the Snowflake or Leucoion (literally, " White Violet ").

## NOTE II.

### ON THE AZALEA VISCOSA.

I was much pleased to see my observations on the Azalea as a fly-catcher confirmed by a subsequent paragraph (October 3, 1874,) in the *Gardeners' Chronicle.* It is interesting, and I now reprint it.

#### AZALEA VISCOSA A FLY CATCHER.

Under this heading Mr. W. W. Bailey gives the following observations in the current number of the *American Naturalist:*—

"The many curious observations published of late in regard to vegetable fly-catchers have opened my eyes to such phenomena as are presented in my forest walks. As is well known to all botanists, our sweet swamp Azalea (Azalea viscosa) has its corolla covered on the outside with innumerable clammy and glandular hairs. Each hair is a prolongation of the cuticle, and is surmounted by a purple and globular band. In the bud these hairs appear to cover the whole surface of the flower, but when the corolla expands they are seen to occupy the midrib of the petals as well as the tube of the corolla. These glandular hairs are efficacious fly-catchers, but what the object is in thus securing insect prey I will not pretend to state. I have been amusing myself, if any such apparently cruel occupation can be considered entertaining, in watching the capture of flies by the Azaleas. When I first brought the flowers home, many small insects, as winged ants, were entrapped amidst the hairs. These have remained alive several days, still vainly struggling for freedom. As the house-flies are abundant in my room, it occurred to me that I might extirpate the pests, and at the same time learn something of the process of insect-catching. I have not noticed that the powerful fragrance of the blossoms attracts the house-fly, although I have no doubt that it does the smaller insects. It seemed to be accidental when the house-flies were captured. I exposed a number of buds and fully-opened blossoms on a sunny window-sill thronged with flies. It was not many minutes before I had several captives. A mere touch of a fly's leg to the glutinous hairs was sufficient for his detention. A struggle only made matters worse, as other legs were by this means brought in contact with the glands. These emit long glairy threads, which fasten to the hairs of the flies' legs. They may be drawn out to a great length and tenuity, still retaining their strength. If two buds are pressed together, and then drawn apart, innumerable threads may be seen to bind them. There is a complete network of them between the various glands. They will confine the strongest fly; he is at once held like Gulliver among the Lilliputians. Under the microscope the legs of the fly are seen to be covered with the secretion, which is perfectly white and transparent. In one attempt to escape, a house-fly lifted a flower bodily from the window-sill, perhaps a quarter of an inch, but at once sank back exhausted amidst the hairs. One, after long efforts, escaped, but seemed incapable of using its legs; it flew away readily. In one instance I have found the dried remains of a small insect embedded amidst the hairs, but cannot say whether its juices were in any way absorbed by the plant. If such assimilation takes place, what is its purpose? Can this phenomenon of fly-catching be accidental, or is some nice purpose concealed in it? I merely state the facts as I have observed them; perhaps others can supply further information."

## NOTE III.

### ON THE SOLANUM TRIBE.

It is very curious to compare the two following passages of two great masters of style—Ruskin and Michelet—both writing of the tribe to which belongs the Tomato. Ruskin, in *The Queen of the Air*, p. 91, says:—

"Next, in the Potato, we have the scarcely innocent underground stem of one of a tribe set aside for evil, having the deadly nightshade for its queen, and including the henbane, the witch's mandrake, and the worst natural curse of modern civilisation—tobacco. And the strange thing about this tribe is, that though thus set aside for evil, they are not a group distinctly separate from those that are happier in function. There is nothing in other tribes of plants like the form of the bean blossom; but there is another family with forms and structure closely connected with this venomous one. Examine the purple and yellow bloom of the common hedge Nightshade;— you will find it constructed exactly like some of the forms of the Cyclamen; and getting this clue, you will find at last the whole poisonous and terrible group to be —sisters of the Primulas.

"The nightshades are, in fact, primroses with a curse upon them, and a sign set in their petals by which the deadly and condemned flower may always be known from the innocent one,—that the stamens of the nightshades are between the lobes, and of the primulas opposite the lobes of the corolla."

Now for M. Michelet. In *La Sorcière*, p. 119, he writes of the herbs used by the witches:—

"Ce que nous savons le mieux de leur médecine, c'est qu'elles employaient beaucoup, pour les usages les plus divers, pour calmer, pour stimuler, une grande famille de plantes, équivoques, fort dangereuses, qui rendirent les plus grands services. On les nomme avec raison, les *Consolantes* (Solanées).

"Famille immense et populaire, dont la plupart des espèces sont surabondantes, sous nos pieds, aux haies, partout. Famille, tellement nombreuse, qu'un seul de ses genres a huit cents espèces. Rien de plus facile à trouver, rien de plus vulgaire. Mais ces plantes sont la plupart d'un emploi fort hasardeux. Il a fallu de l'audace pour en préciser les doses, l'audace peut-être du génie.

"Prenons par en bas l'échelle ascendante de leurs énergies. Les premières sont tout simplement potagères et bonnes à manger (les aubergines, les tomates, mal appelées pommes d'amour). D'autres de ces innocentes sont le calme et la douceur même, les molènes (bouillon blanc), si utiles aux fomentations.

I

"Vous rencontrez au dessus une plante déjà suspecte, que plusieurs croyaient un poison, la plante miellée d'abord, amère ensuite, qui semble dire le mot de Jonathas : 'J'ai mangé un peu de miel, et voilà pourquoi je meurs.' Mais cette mort est utile, c'est l'amortissement de la douleur. La douce-amère, c'est son nom, dut être le premier essai de l'homœopathie hardie, qui, peu à peu, s'éleva aux plus dangereux poisons. La légère irritation, les picotements qu'elle donne purent la désigner pour remède des maladies dominantes de ces temps, celles de la peau."

Speaking of magical herbs reminds one of the "moly," which Mercury gives to Ulysses, and which enabled him to withstand the enchantments of Circe. This "moly" with its white blossom is particularly well known to me, for, when I first came to my present house, the wood near the lodge was so full of it that it seemed as if a dinner of onions was for ever being cooked: I found it exceedingly hard to eradicate. "Moly" is none other than the Garlic, and Circe had apparently the same objection to it as had the wife of the Merchant of Bagdad in the *Arabian Nights*.

By the way, what could Mr. Tennyson have been thinking of when he describes his lotus-eaters as

"Propt on beds of amaranth and *moly*"?

Another poet too, now a well-known divine, once spoke of

"—souls that pure and holy
Live and love and prosper well,
Leaning aye on myrrh and *moly*,
Melilote and asphodel."

## NOTE IV.

#### ON THE SUNFLOWER OF THE CLASSICS.

I have been much puzzled to know what was the Sunflower of classical story,—in other words, what was the flower into which, according to the legend, Clytie was so sadly changed.

I had always supposed, as nearly every one supposes, that it was what *we* call the Sunflower (the Helianthus), with its upright stem and large radiated disc. But, first of all, I found, as a matter of fact, that the Helianthus does *not* follow the course of the Sun, and that various blossoms of the same plant may at the same time be facing in different directions. And then I found, what of course was fatal, that the Helianthus is not a European plant at all, and first came to us from North America.

Having consulted *Notes and Queries* in vain, I determined to look into the matter more closely, as it seemed to me a rather curious question.

If the Sunflower of the Classics was not the Helianthus, and if this, as I imagine, only obtained its name from its flowers, which in some way resemble the old pictures of the Sun, could it be the plant we know as *Heliotrope?* The name of course means "turning Sunward," but again the name is no guide to us; the scented flowers of the Heliotrope do not, so far as I know, turn to the Sun, and in any case the plant is of Peruvian and not of European origin.

I then fell back upon the classical authors themselves. I got nothing very distinct from Theophrastus, and moreover it is Ovid, to whom we chiefly owe our knowledge of the story. He tells us that when her lover Phœbus left her, poor Clytie "still gazed on the face of the departing god, and bent her looks on him. It is said that she remained rooted to the ground; of her fresh bloom ('color'), part is turned by livid pallor into bloodless leaves, on part a blush remains, and a flower most like a Violet has covered all her face. Held firmly by the root, she still turns to the Sun she loves, and, changed herself, she keeps her love unchanged."

Pliny says the Heliotropium "turns with the Sun, in cloudy weather even, so great is its sympathy with that luminary. At night, as though in regret, it closes its blue flowers."

What then can this flower be, a blue flower, which turns towards the Sun?

I next examined the magnificent volumes of Sibthorp's *Flora Græca*. There is there indeed a European "Heliotropium," "Heliotropium supinum," but this surely cannot be the flower of Clytie; the blossom is quite insignificant ("flore minimo") and *white*. Then there are two Crotons (Tinctorium and Villosum) which are also locally called Heliotropium, and which grow in Crete and Lemnos ("ex quâ paratur Tournesol"), but their flowers again are hardly more noticeable and are *yellow*.

Foiled at every point, I thought I would at least see what in *England* was the traditional Sunflower, but I am hardly any wiser.

Gerarde says that Valerius Cordius calls the dwarf Cistus Helianthemum, and Solis flos or Sunne-flower.

He quotes Pliny as calling it also "Heliocalliden, or the Beautie of the Sunne;" and adds, "which if it be the Sunneflower, yet there is another of the same name, but which may be taken for the right it is hard to tell (but that experience teacheth us), seeing Plinie is so breefe."

Gerarde has also a chapter on the "Tornesole," and says, "there be five sorts of Tornesole, differing one from another in many notable points, as in greatnesse and smallnesse, in colour of flowers, in forme and shape," and then he describes the varieties of "Tornesoles" or "Heliotropium."

He says, "the Græcians call it Heliotropium;"—"it is named Heliotropium, not because it is turned about at the daily motion of the sunne, but by reason it flowreth in the summer solstice, at which time the sunne being farthest gone from the equinoctiale circle, returneth to the same;" but he adds that the French and Italians call it "Turnesol," and says, "it is also called Herba Clitiæ, whereof the poet hath these verses,

> "'Herba velut Clitiæ semper petit obvia solem,
> Sic pia mens Christum, quo prece spectet, habet.'"

Cowley's Sunflower is called in a foot-note Chrysanthemum Peruvianum, but is probably a form of Helianthus. The flower is supposed to speak, and claims to be a *child* of the Sun, for,

> "My orb-like aspect bound with rays
> The very picture of his face displays;

and again,

> "I still adore my sire with prostrate face,
> Turn where he turns, and all his motions trace."

So after all I am as much in the dark as ever. Was the mysterious flower, as some suggest, a Calendula (Marygold), or an Aster? I cannot tell, and only know that neither answers the description. On the whole then I am disposed to wonder whether either Ovid or Pliny knew much more about the matter than ourselves, and I may some day come to doubt whether Clytie was ever turned into a Sunflower at all.[1]

## NOTE V.

### FLOWERS AND THE POETS.

Both the flowers of the garden and what Campbell calls "wildings of nature" have had their bards, and in the case of certain flowers the association with a poet is so strong that the sight of the flower will recall the verse. Of course this is chiefly so as regards the less familiar flowers. No one, not even Sappho, has an exclusive possession in the Rose; but who would care to dispute Shelley's right to the Sensitive Plant, or Wordsworth's to the lesser Celandine? The poets, however, have sometimes more of a love than a knowledge of plants, and Milton talks of the "twisted Eglantine" in confusion between the Sweetbrier and the Honeysuckle.

It is interesting to see the different ways in which

---

[1] One of our very best living authorities on such a subject has sent me the suggestion that the common Salsafy, or possibly the Anagallis, may be the flower, but he adds (agreeing with Gerarde), "the word Heliotropium does not mean a flower which turns to the sun, but which flowers at the solstice."

flowers are treated by the poets. Shakspeare, no doubt, loved them in his way, but after all, there are but few passages in which flowers are used otherwise than as an illustration or an emblem. There are, indeed, Titania's flowered bank, and Perdita's garden, —redolent of herbs and gay with Violets, Primroses, and Daffodils, but where no Gillyflower was allowed to grow,—and poor Ophelia's melancholy blossoms, and the song in *Love's Labour's Lost*, and that is nearly all. Shakspeare often speaks of Roses, but almost always, excepting in the scene at the Temple Gardens, by way of compliment or comparison. The *musk*-rose, indeed, appears in the *Midsummer Night's Dream*, and this Rose, which is now quite unknown to most of us, was evidently a favourite in Elizabethan gardens, for Bacon says of it that, next the white double Violet (which is also almost lost), the musk-rose "yeelds the sweetest smell in the aire."

But Shakspeare's favourite flowers seem to have been the Primrose, the Violet, the Pansy, and, above all, the Cowslip. He must often have recalled his boyish walks in spring along the Avon, and remembered how the low-lying fields of Stratford were all sweet and yellow with the Cowslip. And so it is within a Cowslip's bell that Ariel hides, and Cowslips are Titania's pensioners on whose ears the fairies must hang pearls, and when the fields of France are desolated the "freckled Cowslip" does not grow there any more, and the mole on Imogen's breast is "like the crimson drops i' the bottom of a Cowslip."

Before passing from Shakspeare, I should like to call the attention of the directors or managers of New Place to the absurdity of the garden, which they are supposed to keep up in remembrance of Shakspeare. I chanced to visit it a summer or two ago, and, instead of finding an Elizabethan garden with flowers associated with Shakspeare and his times, I saw little but a wretched ribbon border of starveling Calceolarias, scrubby Pelargoniums, and miserable Perillas. Such a garden is a mockery, and would be more suggestive and more pathetic if left wild to the growths of nature.

If Milton enjoyed more completely the luxury of gardens, it is safe to say that he knew less of separate flowers than Shakspeare. He not only speaks of the Eglantine as "twisted," but he calls the Cowslip "wan," the Violet "glowing," and the Reed "balmy." He makes Roses and Crocuses bloom together in Paradise, and Hyacinths and Roses in the gardens of Hesperus, while Lycid's "laureate hearse" is to be strewn with Primrose and Woodbine, Daffodil and Jessamine. Paradise and the gardens of Hesperus are, of course, ideal gardens, which may be superior to our times and seasons, but the same excuse cannot hold good for the flowers of the "Lycidas," and it is tolerably clear that Milton's special knowledge was somewhat vague. But, on the other hand, what a sensuous pleasure he has in gardens! He is not thinking of Elizabethan gardens, but such gardens as he may have seen in Italy, or read of in Tasso or Boccaccio. The west winds fling around the cedared alleys sweet smells of Nard and Cassia, or the covert is of inwoven shade of Laurel and Myrtle fenced by Acanthus and odorous shrubs. The rich rhythm of his lines seems to breathe perfume and delight.

And the reason why, in later years at least, the scent

rather than the sight of flowers was dear to Milton, is known to all of us, for has he not himself told us how,

> "Not to me returns
> Day, or the sweet approach of ev'n or morn,
> Or *sight of vernal bloom or summer's rose?*"

He could still drink in the perfumed air of gardens, though only memory could recall the form and colour of those flowers, which he would never see again.[1]

Only one English poet has surpassed Milton in his love of gardens. Like Milton he probably knew little of particular flowers, but he revelled in the scent and colour of Roses and of Lilies. It is Andrew Marvell; who, it is to be feared, is far less remembered than he deserves to be. Marvell's gardens are all of the true English character, and his description of Lord Fairfax's, though somewhat quaint and fanciful, has many touches as natural as they are graceful. That the flowers should stand on parade, like soldiers, through the day, and fold up at night in tents, in which bees remain as sentinels, is a far-fetched conceit enough; but nothing can be better than many of his lines. Was it his own garden at

---

[1] I remember how years ago I was struck with a beautiful little poem about a blind man, written by Mr. James Payn, the well-known novelist. The lines are quite worth repeating, and will be new to many:—

> "There an old man, far in his wintry time,
> Sits under his porch, while the roses climb;
> But the breath of its sweetness is all he knows
> Of the glory about the fair round rose;
> The lilies that sway in the brook beneath,
> So cold and white in the beauty of death,
> Are to him far less than the rushes tall
> When the wind is bowing them one and all,
> Like the voice of nature so soft and kind,
> That whispers how fair she is to *the blind*."

Highgate of which he thought, when he spoke of the garden in which Sylvio's fawn was wont to hide?

> "I have a garden of my own,
> But so with roses overgrown
> And lilies, that you would it guess
> To be a little wilderness."

Cowley's love of a garden was of quite another kind. He cared about it as a horticulturist, and knew the various plants and their qualities; but he never luxuriated in it like Milton or like Marvell. His elaborate poem is interesting, if only to show the flowers that were cultivated in his day, and it is curious to find the Tomato (or love-apple) grown for beauty and not for use, and the *Canna Indica*, which is hardly common with us even now, mentioned as among the ordinary flowers of his time. On the whole, however, there are very few lines of Cowley about flowers (we are not speaking of anything else) which are worth quoting or remembering.

Herrick's use of flowers is very different. He loved them, no doubt, and is always talking about them, and making them useful.

> "He twists his coronals of fancy
> Out of all blossoms,"

if I may so misapply a line from Lord Houghton's *Letters of Youth*. He makes moralities out of Daffodils, and compliments from Carnations, and warnings from Rosebuds. Charming as many of his poems about flowers are, it is impossible not to feel that the motive of the poem is not the flower itself, but the Anthea or Sappho or Julia, to whom the flower is to teach a lesson of the power of love or the uncertainty of life.

It is, of course, impossible to speak of all the poets who have written about flowers, for probably the list would include them all; but the five I have mentioned are perhaps the most characteristic, though there are memorable lines in Chaucer, Spenser, Burns, and Keats, and more especially in Wordsworth.

From Byron there is singularly little to quote; but no English poet has given so perfect a description of a garden as has Shelley in "The Sensitive Plant." How delicately he paints each flower, and how he makes us see them all, as we tread with him

> "The sinuous paths of lawn and of moss
> Which led through the garden along and across;
> Some open at once to the sun and the breeze,
> Some lost among bowers of blossoming trees."

Of living English poets perhaps Mr. Tennyson alone shows any real love for flowers. And this love is scarcely shown so much in the well-known song in "Maud" as by little touches here and there—the "long green box of mignonette" which the miller's daughter has set on her casement edge,—the "wild marsh-marygold" which "shines like fire in swamps" for the happy May Queen,—or the water-lilies which blossom round the island of Shalott. And who can forget the stanza in "In Memoriam"?—

> "Bring orchis, bring the foxglove spire,
> The little speedwell's darling blue,
> Deep tulips dasht with fiery dew,
> Laburnums, dropping-wells of fire."

Of American poets, Mr. Longfellow has, rather strangely, written nothing very memorable about flowers;

but there are some pretty verses of Mr. Bryant's, and an occasional good line of Mr. Emerson's, as where he speaks of the Gentian as "blue-eyed pet of blue-eyed lover."

As we once again look round upon the poets that have sung, it is clear that their favourite flowers have been the Rose and the Daisy,—the one recalling all the delights of the summer garden, the other all the freshness of the open field,—the one loved for its beauty, the other cherished for its constancy.

> "The rose has but a summer reign,
> The daisy never dies;"

says Montgomery, in one of the best known of his poems. Cowslips, Violets, Daffodils, and Pansies are probably the next favourites. Painters have done more for Lilies than the poets have; and Carnations and the later flowers of the year have never made much place for themselves in the poetry of England. The English garden of to-day still awaits its laureate, and, except where, in Mr. Allingham's "Therania,"

> "Vase and plot burn scarlet, gold and azure,"

I scarcely know of a description of modern "bedding-out," and sincerely hope that the present fashion may disappear before the thankless task is undertaken.

## THE END.

RICHARD CLAY AND SONS, LIMITED, LONDON AND BUNGAY.

www.ingramcontent.com/pod-product-compliance
Lightning Source LLC
Chambersburg PA
CBHW021936160426
43195CB00011B/1104